INVESTIGATIONS **3**

IN NUMBER, DATA, AND SPACE®

STUDENT ACTIVITY BOOK

PEARSON

TERC

Glenview, Illinois • Boston, Massachusetts • Chandler, Arizona • New York, New York

The Investigations curriculum was developed by TERC, Cambridge, MA.

This material is based on work supported by the National Science Foundation ("NSF") under Grant No. ESI-0095450. Any opinions, findings, and conclusions or recommendations expressed in this material are those of the author(s) and do not necessarily reflect the views of the National Science Foundation.

ISBN-13: 978-0-328-86030-2
ISBN-10: 0-328-86030-1

9 19

UNIT 1 Understanding Equal Groups

UNIT 1 CONTENTS (continued)

UNIT 2 Graphs and Line Plots

UNIT 2 CONTENTS (continued)

UNIT 3 Travel Stories and Collections

INVESTIGATION 2

INVESTIGATION 3

CONTENTS

INVESTIGATION 5

UNIT 4 Perimeter, Area, and Polygons

INVESTIGATION 1

UNIT 4 CONTENTS (continued)

UNIT 5 Cube Patterns, Arrays, and Multiples of 10

INVESTIGATION 1

CONTENTS

INVESTIGATION 2

UNIT 6 Fair Shares and Fractions on Number Lines

INVESTIGATION 1

UNIT 7 How Many Miles?

UNIT 8 Larger Numbers and Multi-Step Problems

UNIT 8 CONTENTS (*continued*)

Understanding
Equal Groups

Understanding
Equal Groups

NAME

DATE

Wheels, Apples, and Days

Solve the problems and show your solutions.

 1 There are 5 cars parked in the driveway. How many wheels are there altogether?

 2 I have 3 bags of apples. Each bag has 6 apples. How many apples do I have?

 3 My birthday is 3 weeks away. Each week has 7 days. How many days away is my birthday?

Ongoing Review

 4 $8 + 8 + 8 =$ _____

    Ⓐ 16   Ⓑ 23   Ⓒ 24   Ⓓ 25

NOTE

Students solve multiplication problems.
 Solving Multiplication Problems

NAME

DATE

Things That Come in Groups

Talk with family members—or look around your home or in a store—to find things that come in groups of 2 to 10. Write the name of each item and the quantity the item comes in.

Item	Comes in Groups of This Many

NOTE

Students have been solving multiplication problems about things that come in groups of a certain amount. For example, there are 4 wheels on a car, juice boxes are packaged in groups of 3, and so on. Help your child find things at home, outside, or in a store that come in equal groups.

MWI Solving Multiplication Problems

About the Mathematics in This Unit

Dear Family,

Our class is starting a new mathematics unit about multiplication and division called *Understanding Equal Groups*. During this unit, students develop an understanding that we use multiplication to combine a number of equal groups and that we use division to split a quantity into equal groups. By the end of Grade 3, it is expected that students will be fluent with multiplication combinations up to 10×10.

Throughout the unit, students work toward the following goals:

BENCHMARKS/GOALS	EXAMPLES
Demonstrate an understanding of multiplication and division as involving equal groups.	Here are 3 stars. Each star has 5 points. There are 15 points in all. $3 \times 5 = 15$
Solve multiplication and related division problems using skip counting or known multiplication facts.	Ms. Wilson's class is counting around the class by 4s. What number will the 8th student say? 4, 8, 12, 16, 20, 24, 28, 32
	$4 \times 8 = (4 \times 4) + (4 \times 4)$ $4 \times 8 = 16 + 16$ $4 \times 8 = 32$
Interpret and use multiplication and division notation.	There are 35 flowers. Gina wants to put them in bouquets of 5 flowers each. She can make 7 bouquets. $35 \div 5 = 7$

About the Mathematics in This Unit

BENCHMARKS/GOALS	EXAMPLES
Demonstrate fluency with the ×1, ×2, ×5 and ×10 multiplication facts.	5×6 Start with _____

This unit is the first of three units in Grade 3 that focus on multiplication and division. Later this year, students will solve multiplication and division problems with larger numbers.

In our math class, students spend time discussing problems in depth and are asked to share their reasoning and solutions. It is most important that children accurately and efficiently solve math problems in ways that make sense to them. At home, encourage your child to explain his or her math thinking to you. Please look for more information and activities about equal groups that will be sent home in the coming weeks.

NAME

DATE

Fingers and Eyes

Solve the problems and show your solutions.

1 There are 4 people sitting at my table. Each person has 5 fingers on each hand. How many fingers are there altogether?

2 There are 8 people in my group. Each person has 2 eyes. How many eyes are there altogether?

3 Write a story problem that represents 4×3.

Ongoing Review

4 $5 \times 3 = $ _____

Ⓐ 9　　　Ⓑ 12　　　Ⓒ 15　　　Ⓓ 25

NOTE

Students write and solve multiplication problems.
MWI Solving Multiplication Problems

NAME

DATE

Pictures of Things That Come in Groups

In class, we've been drawing pictures of things that come in groups. Choose another item that comes in groups. On a piece of paper:

1 Draw a picture of several groups of the item.

2 Write sentences about the three pieces of mathematical information in your picture.

3 Then write the multiplication equation that describes your picture.

Here is an example:

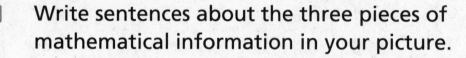

Here are 6 cars
Each car has 4 wheels.
There are 24 wheels in all.

$6 \times 4 = 24$

Choose ANOTHER item that comes in groups and follow the same steps. On another piece of paper draw a picture, write sentences, and write an equation.

NOTE

Students represent and solve problems involving multiplication.
MWI Solving Multiplication Problems

Related Activities to Try at Home

Dear Family,

The activities below are related to the mathematics in the multiplication and division unit *Understanding Equal Groups*. You can use the activities to enrich your child's mathematical learning experience.

Things That Come in Groups In math class, your child has been investigating things that come in equal groups. Some examples are shown below.

Eggs come in a carton of 12. Spiders have 8 legs.	Juice boxes come in packages of 3. Cars have 4 tires.

Your family may continue to keep track of what kinds of things come in groups and how many come in a group. Are there some numbers for which many examples exist? Are there some that are very hard to find?

Skip Counting One way that your child has explored multiplication is by skip counting. You can continue to build on this work by asking questions such as the following:

○ What number would we land on if we counted by 3s (3, 6, 9, and so on) and everyone in our family said one number?

○ What would happen if we counted by 3s and everyone had two turns?

○ How many people would have to count by 3s to reach 27? You can count off by 3s to check.

Related Activities to Try at Home

Multiplication and Division Problems in Everyday Situations Your child has also been working on understanding multiplication and division situations. Encourage your child to think about situations that involve equal groups as opportunities arise.

○ How many legs are on the 7 pigeons we saw in the park?

○ How many toes are under the table while we eat dinner?

○ If we share this batch of cookies equally, how many cookies will each person in our family get?

○ Five pencils cost $1.00. How many pencils can we buy with $4.00?

Picture Problems

For each problem, write a multiplication equation, solve the problem, and show your solution.

 There are 10 apples in a basket.
Each apple has 4 worms.
How many worms do the apples have in all?

2 There are 4 sports bags.
Each bag has 9 balls inside.
How many balls are there in all?

Picture Problems

For each problem, write a multiplication equation, solve the problem, and show your solution.

 Alan sees 6 cars.
Each car has 4 wheels.
How many wheels does Alan see?

 Mia has 5 packs of juice boxes.
There are 6 juice boxes in each pack.
How many juice boxes does she have?

Picture Problems

For each problem, write a multiplication equation, solve the problem, and show your solution.

5 Rosi has 3 bags of marbles.
There are 8 marbles in each bag.
How many marbles does Rosi have?

6 Jack drew 7 hexagons.
Hexagons have 6 sides.
How many sides did Jack draw in all?

NAME   DATE

Multiplication Practice

For each problem, write a multiplication equation, solve the problem, and show your solution.

 There are 8 cows in a field.
Each cow has 4 legs.
How many legs are there?

 Inez drew 7 stars.
Each star had 5 points.
How many points did she draw?

3 Chris bought 4 packs of pencils.
There are 6 pencils in each pack.
How many pencils did he buy?

NOTE

Students practice solving multiplication problems.
MWI Solving Multiplication Problems

About Mathematics Homework

Dear Family,

Homework is an important link between learning inside and outside school. Homework assignments provide reinforcement of the work students do in math class. Here are some suggestions for making the homework experience successful for your child:

- Set a regular time every day for homework, and establish a quiet place for your child to work (whether at home, in an afterschool program, or some other location).

- Establish a system for bringing homework to and from school. Use an assignment book, a homework folder, or other organizational tools.

- Students will bring home the materials and directions needed for homework activities. Certain materials will be used throughout the year. Because these materials will be sent home only once, please help your child find a safe place to store them so that your child can easily locate them when needed. If your child regularly does homework in more than one place, please let me know so we can talk about how to obtain the necessary materials.

- In our math class, students explore problems in depth and share their reasoning and solutions. It is important that students solve math problems by using problem-solving methods that are meaningful to them. At home, encourage your child to explain his or her strategies and mathematical ideas to you.

About Mathematics Homework

When your child asks you for help in solving a problem, ask questions such as these:

○ What are you trying to figure out?
○ Does this remind you of other problems?
○ What part of the problem do you already know how to solve?
○ Where is a good place to start?
○ What have you figured out so far?
○ Would drawing a picture or diagram help?
○ How can I help you (without telling you an answer)?

If you would like to share any thoughts with me about how your child is approaching a homework task, please feel free to send me a note. If an assignment seems too difficult, too confusing, or perhaps too easy, please let me know so that I can address the issue. I look forward to working with you throughout the year.

Chapters, Slices, and Miles

Write multiplication equations, solve the problems, and show your solutions.

1 There are 3 books in a series. Each book has 9 chapters. If I read all of the books, how many chapters will I read altogether?

2 I have 4 pizzas. Each pizza has 8 slices. How many slices are there altogether?

3 George ran for 6 days. He ran 5 miles each day. How many miles did he run altogether?

Ongoing Review

4 Choose the equation that goes with this story. Orange juice comes in packs of 4 cans. I have 5 packs of orange juice. How many cans of orange juice do I have?

Ⓐ $20 \times 4 = ?$ Ⓒ $9 \times 6 = ?$

Ⓑ $5 \times 4 = ?$ Ⓓ $5 \times 20 = ?$

NOTE

Students solve multiplication problems.
MWI Solving Multiplication Problems

NAME

DATE

More Picture Problems

For each problem, write a multiplication equation, solve the problem, and show your solution.

  In Kelley's picture, there are 6 shirts. Each shirt has 6 buttons. How many buttons are there altogether?

  Pilar brought 5 packs of crayons. There are 8 crayons in each pack. How many crayons are there altogether?

3 Benjamin drew a picture of some dogs. Each dog has 4 legs. There are 28 legs in the picture. How many dogs did he draw?

NOTE

Students solve multiplication problems.
MWI Solving Multiplication Problems

© Pearson Education 3

NAME   DATE

Groups, Groups, Everywhere!

For each problem, write a multiplication equation, solve the problem, and show your solution.

 There are 4 wheels on a car.
How many wheels are on 5 cars?

 There are 2 wings on a bird.
How many wings are on 6 birds?

 There are 8 legs on a spider.
How many legs are on 3 spiders?

Ongoing Review

4   Which multiplication expression equals 30?

Ⓐ 4×5 Ⓒ 10×2

Ⓑ 5×6 Ⓓ 7×4

NOTE

Students solve multiplication problems.
MWI Solving Multiplication Problems

NAME

DATE

Saving Nickels

Solve these problems and show your solutions.

 Adam decided to save a nickel every day. How much money did Adam have after 2 days?

 How much money did Adam have after 5 days?

 How much money did he have after 10 days?

 How much money did he have after 20 days?

NOTE

Students practice multiplying by 5s. All four problems are related to one another, and students may use the answer to one problem to help them find the answer to another.
MWI Related Multiplication Problems

Counting Around by 2s, 5s, and 10s

Students in Mrs. Hamilton's homeroom are counting around the class by 2s, 5s, and 10s. For each problem, draw a picture or write a multiplication equation to represent the problem. Solve the problem and show your solution.

 Students are counting around the class by 5s. What number would the 3rd person say?

2 Students are counting around the class by 2s. What number would the 7th person say?

3 Students are counting around the class by 10s. What number would the 9th person say?

NOTE

Students practice skip counting by 2s, 5s, and 10s.

MWI Skip Counting

Related Problems

Solve the problems in Set A. For each problem, write a multiplication equation, solve the problem, and show your solution.

Set A

 Triangles have 3 sides.
How many sides do 7 triangles have?

 Hexagons have 6 sides.
How many sides do 7 hexagons have?

Related Problems

Solve the problems in Set B. For each problem, complete the multiplication equation, solve the problem, and show your solution.

Set B

1 Nancy and Philip were finding multiples on their skip counting charts. They circled 42 on the 6s chart. How many jumps of 6 did they take to get to 42?

$$\underline{\hspace{3cm}} \times 6 = 42$$

2 Deondra and Kenji circled 42 on the 3s chart. How many jumps of 3 did they take to get to 42? Show how you got your answer.

$$\underline{\hspace{3cm}} \times 3 = 42$$

Related Problems

Solve the problems in Set C and Set D. For each problem, write a multiplication equation, solve the problem, and show your solution.

Set C

1 Oscar bought juice boxes that come in packages of 6. He bought 5 packs. How many juice boxes did he buy?

2 Pilar bought 8 packs of juice boxes. How many juice boxes did she buy?

Set D

1 Deondra noticed 7 children outside her house, each riding a tricycle. How many wheels were there altogether?

2 Two more children rode up on tricycles. How many wheels were there then?

Choose one set (A, B, C, or D) and explain how the first problem could help you solve the second problem. Write your answer on another sheet of paper.

Multiplication Match

1 Draw lines to match each problem to its solution.

There are 4 children.
Each child saves 5 dimes.
How many dimes do they save in all?

Each child has 3.

There are 3 children. Each child has
the same number of balloons.
There is a total of 9 balloons.
How many balloons does each child have?

15 in all

There are 5 children.
Each child has the same number of books.
Together they have 20 books.
How many books does each child have?

20 in all

There are 5 children. Each child has
3 markers. How many markers do
they have altogether?

Each child has 4.

Ongoing Review

2 What is 6 × 4?

Ⓐ 10   Ⓑ 24   Ⓒ 32   Ⓓ 40

NOTE

Students solve multiplication problems.
MWI **Solving Multiplication Problems**

NAME   DATE

More Related Problems

Solve these problems and show your solutions.

1 $3 \times 7 =$ _____

2 $6 \times 7 =$ _____

3 $3 \times 5 =$ _____

4 $6 \times 5 =$ _____

5 $4 \times 6 =$ _____

6 $9 \times 6 =$ _____

NOTE

Students use what they know to solve multiplication problems. For example, the answer to the first problem may help them solve the second problem.

MWI Related Multiplication Problems

Counting Around by 3s and 6s

1 One day Ms. Johnson's class counted around the room by 6s. The 5th person said 30.

The next day they counted around by 3s. Some students in the class said they knew that this time the 5th person would say 15.

Use a number line, a 100 Chart, or a picture to show if that is true.

Counting Around by 3s and 6s

2 Ms. Ross owns an apple orchard. She was making bags that each held 6 apples. In order to fill up 5 bags, she used 30 apples.

The next day she was filling bags that held 3 apples. She knew that this time she would need only 15 apples to fill up 5 bags.

Use a number line, 100 Chart, or picture to show whether that is true.

NAME   DATE

Represent and Solve Addition Problems

For each problem, write an equation, solve the problem, and show your solution.

 At a water park, Ingrid counted 105 children with dark hair and 30 children with blond hair. How many children did she count?

 Alex walked 150 feet from the porch to the sidewalk. Then he walked 68 feet to the car. How many feet did he walk in all?

 Plane A has 137 passengers. Plane B has 73 passengers. What is the total number of passengers on both planes?

 Rachel made 175 chocolate chip cookies and 45 sugar cookies for a bake sale. How many cookies did she make in all?

NOTE

Students solve addition story problems.
MWI Addition Strategies: Adding by Place

NAME

DATE

How Many Legs?

Solve the problems and show your solutions.

 1 Cats have 4 legs.

How many legs are on 3 cats?

How many legs are on 7 cats?

How many legs are on 9 cats?

 2 Insects have 6 legs.

How many legs are on 3 insects?

How many legs are on 5 insects?

How many legs are on 8 insects?

NAME

DATE

What's the Difference?

For each problem, write an equation, solve the problem, and show your solution.

1 Malcolm has collected 140 baseball cards.
He gives 15 cards to his little brother.
How many baseball cards does he have left?

2 A florist has 123 flowers for sale.
At the end of the day, the florist has 53 flowers left.
How many flowers did the florist sell?

3 An average adult female giraffe is about 168 inches tall.
At birth, a baby giraffe is about 72 inches tall.
About how much taller is an adult female giraffe than
a baby giraffe?

4 Tamika counted 154 people at a 4ᵗʰ of July picnic.
Of those she counted, 67 were **NOT** wearing red shirts.
How many people were wearing red shirts?

NOTE

Students solve subtraction story problems.
MWI Subtraction Situations

© Pearson Education 3

NAME   DATE

Spiders, Cats, and People

Solve the problems and show your solutions.

In an old house, there live some spiders, cats, and people.

| Cats have 4 legs. | Spiders have 8 legs. | People have 2 legs. |

1 In one room, there are 4 cats and 3 spiders. How many legs are there altogether?

2 In another room, there are 3 people and 5 cats. How many legs are there altogether?

3 In another room, there are 16 legs. What could be in that room? Can you find more than one possibility? Explain your thinking.

NOTE

Students practice multiplying by 2s, 4s, and 8s.
MWI Learning Multiplication Facts

How Many Towers?

Solve each problem.

1 How many 3s are there in 30?

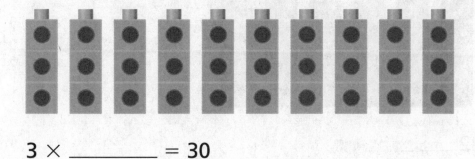

$3 \times$ _____ $= 30$

2 How many 5s are there in 45?

$5 \times$ _____ $= 45$

NOTE

Students solve multiplication problems.
MWI Skip Counting

How Many Towers?

3 How many 4s are there in 32?

$4 \times ? = 32$ _____

4 How many 6s are in 36?

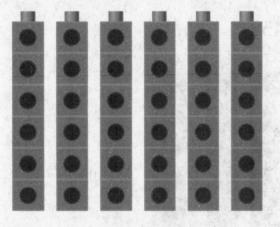

$6 \times ? = 36$ _____

Ongoing Review

5 If I start at 0 and count by 6s, which number will I **NOT** land on?

(A) 6   (B) 24   (C) 30   (D) 32

NAME

DATE

Comic Book Collections

For each problem, write an equation, solve the problem, and show your solution.

1 Adam has 175 comic books. He buys 15 more comic books. How many comic books does he have now?

2 Bridget has 187 comic books and Casawn has 50 comic books. If Casawn and Bridget combine their collections, how many comic books will they have in all?

3 In the Classics section of Denzel's comic book store, there are 153 Western comics and 98 Horror comics for sale. How many total Classics comic books does Denzel have in his store?

NOTE

Students solve addition problems.
MWI Addition Strategies: Adding One Number in Parts

NAME   DATE

Inventory Items

Each week Handy Hardware takes inventory, so the store manager knows how many of each item were sold and how many remain in stock.

For each problem, write an equation, solve the problem, and show your solution.

1 There are 110 light bulbs in stock. During the week, 38 of the light bulbs are sold. How many light bulbs remain in stock?

2 There are 136 bags of mulch in stock. The store sells 81 bags of mulch. How many bags of mulch remain in stock?

3 There are 143 boxes of roofing nails in stock. At the end of the week, 79 boxes remain in stock. How many boxes of roofing nails were sold?

NOTE

Students solve subtraction problems.
MWI **Subtraction Strategies: Subtracting One Number in Parts**

Finding the Area

Use color tiles to completely fill each rectangle.
Label each rectangle with the dimensions.
Then find the area of the rectangle.

1

_____ inches

A

_____ inches

What is the area of the rectangle? _____ square inches

2

_____ inches

B

_____ inches

What is the area of the rectangle? _____ square inches

Finding the Area

Use color tiles to completely fill each rectangle.
Label each rectangle with the dimensions.
Then find the area of the rectangle.

3

_____ inches

C

_____ inches

What is the area of the rectangle? _____ square inches

4

D

_____ inches

_____ inches

What is the area of the rectangle? _____ square inches

Finding the Area

Use tiles to build each rectangle below. Record the dimensions and area of each rectangle.

 5   Rectangle E has one side that is 8 tiles long and another side that is 3 tiles long.

Dimensions: _____ inches by _____ inches

Area: _____ square inches

 6   Rectangle F is 7 tiles by 4 tiles.

Dimensions: _____ inches by _____ inches

Area: _____ square inches

7   Rectangle G is 5 tiles by 5 tiles.

Dimensions: _____ inches by _____ inches

Area: _____ square inches

 8   The dimensions of Rectangle H are 6 tiles by 5 tiles.

Dimensions: _____ inches by _____ inches

Area: _____ square inches

Finding the Area

Complete the table by recording the dimensions and the area of each rectangle.

	Dimensions (in inches)	Area (in square inches)
Example:	5 by 7	35
Rectangle A		
Rectangle B		
Rectangle C		
Rectangle D		
Rectangle E		
Rectangle F		
Rectangle G		
Rectangle H		

NAME _____   DATE _____

What's the Area?

Record the dimensions and the area of each rectangle.

1

Dimensions: _____ by _____

Area: _____ square units

2

Dimensions: _____ by _____

Area: _____ square units

Ongoing Review

3   Which expressions equal 12? Choose the **two** correct answers.

Ⓐ 3 × 4   Ⓑ 12 × 0   Ⓒ 6 × 2   Ⓓ 6 × 6

NOTE

Students find the dimensions and the area of rectangles.
MWI **Area**

NAME   DATE

Making Array Cards

I started to make my own set of Array Cards in class. Now I will finish making my set for homework.

I have the following items:
○ The Array Cards I have made so far
○ The sheets I need to cut to make the rest of the cards
○ The directions on how to make the cards
○ A plastic bag to save the cards in

I need the following items:
○ Scissors
○ Pencil, marker, or crayon

Here are two different ways to figure out the number of squares in a 4 × 6 array.

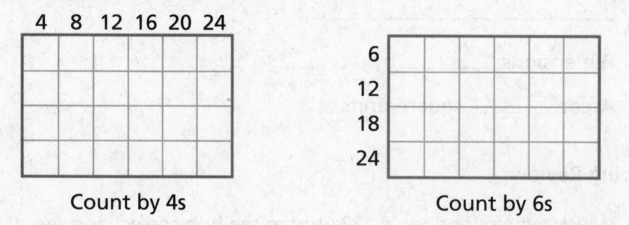

Count by 4s   Count by 6s

NOTE

Students make Array Cards to learn about multiplication and multiplication facts. Ask your child to explain how he or she is figuring out the total number of squares in each array.

MWI Using Arrays to Solve Multiplication Problems

NAME   DATE

How Many Are Left?

For each problem, write an equation, solve the problem, and show your solution.

1 Gina drew 200 pictures of cats. She put 55 of her pictures in an album and gave them to her grandmother as a present. How many cat pictures does Gina have left?

2 Cristobol collected 150 empty pop cans. He used 85 of them to make a sculpture for the school art fair. How many pop cans does he have left?

3 Jackson's father had 173 vinyl records in his music collection. He sold 87 of them at a garage sale. How many vinyl records does he have left?

NOTE

Students solve subtraction problems.
MWI Subtraction Situations

NAME _____ DATE _____

Playing *Factor Pairs*

Let's play *Factor Pairs* together.

I have the following items:

○ A copy of the game rules
○ A list of "Facts I Know" and a list of "Facts I'm Working On"
○ My Array Cards

Here is one of the Array Cards I will be using in the game.

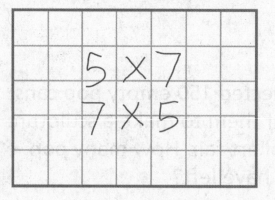

This is how I plan to keep practicing the ones I do **NOT** know.

_____

_____

_____

_____

NOTE

The game "Factor Pairs" is designed to help your child learn multiplication facts. As you play with your child, ask questions about how he or she is figuring out the number of squares on each Array Card.

MWI **Using Arrays to Solve Multiplication Problems**

NAME

DATE

What's the Area?

Find the area of each rectangle.

1   2 units

8 units

Dimensions: _____ by _____

Area: _____ square units

2   4 units

4 units

Dimensions: _____ by _____

Area: _____ square units

NOTE

Students find the area of rectangles.
MWI **Area**

NAME _____ DATE _____

Spots and Stripes

Solve each problem.

1. This butterfly has 6 spots on each wing.
How many spots are on
5 butterflies like this one? _____

2. This fish has 5 black stripes.
How many stripes are on
8 fish like this one? _____

3. This frog has 7 spots.
How many spots are on
10 frogs like this one? _____

4. This zebra has 9 black stripes.
How many stripes are on
3 zebras like this one? _____

5. This ladybug has 4 spots.
How many spots are on
7 ladybugs like this one? _____

NOTE

Students solve multiplication problems.
MWI Solving Multiplication Problems

NAME

DATE

Practicing with Multiplication Cards

Help me practice with my Multiplication Cards.

I have the following items:
o A copy of the directions
o My Multiplication Cards from school or 6 sheets
   to make new ones

Here is the front and back of one Multiplication
Card.

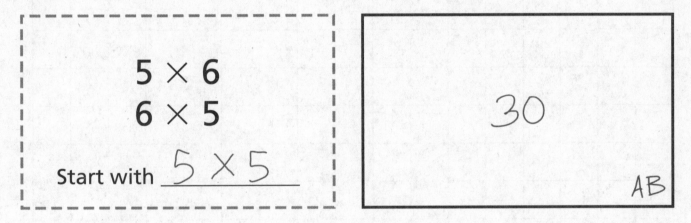

$$5 \times 6$$
$$6 \times 5$$

Start with __5 × 5__

30

AB

NOTE

Students practice learning multiplication facts with products up to 50.
MWI **Learning Multiplication Facts**

Learning Multiplication Facts

Dear Family,

To develop good computation strategies, students need to become fluent with the multiplication facts to 10 × 10, often known as "multiplication facts" or "multiplication tables." Students are expected to know the 2s, 5s, and 10s facts at the end of this unit, and the remaining facts up to 10 × 10 by the end of Unit 5.

It is important for students to recognize that problems such as 8 × 3 and 3 × 8 have the same product. Encourage students to "turn around" a multiplication fact if that makes the problem easier to solve. For example, your child may find it easier to remember the product of 3 × 8 than that of 8 × 3.

In school, students are sorting a set of Multiplication Cards into "Facts I Know" and "Facts I'm Working On." They write clues on their Multiplication Cards to help them learn the facts that are difficult for them. Students use facts that they know that are close to the facts they are solving and then adjust to find the product. Here are some examples.

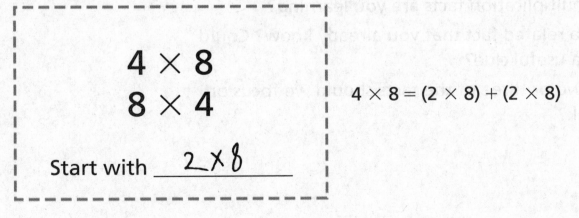

4 × 8
8 × 4

Start with ___2 × 8___

4 × 8 = (2 × 8) + (2 × 8)

Learning Multiplication Facts

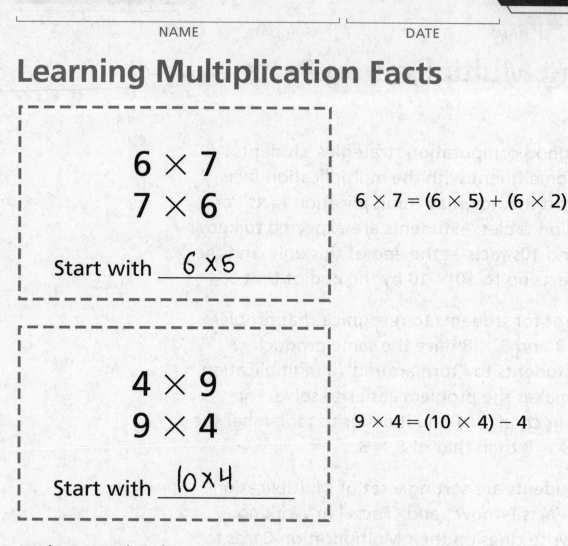

6 × 7
7 × 6

Start with _____6 × 5_____

$6 × 7 = (6 × 5) + (6 × 2)$

4 × 9
9 × 4

Start with _____10 × 4_____

$9 × 4 = (10 × 4) − 4$

As they use the clues to practice, students gradually come to know the facts that are difficult for them. To help your child learn the multiplication facts, ask your child questions such as the following:

o Which multiplication facts are you learning?

o Is there a related fact that you already know? Could that be a useful clue?

o Which two or three of the facts should we focus on this week?

NAME _____ DATE _____

Money Sense: Cents and Dollars

Fill in the blanks to make combinations of three amounts
that add up to one dollar or that add up to two dollars.

Examples:

25¢ + 34¢ + 41¢ = $1 (100 cents)
80¢ + 35¢ + 85¢ = $2 (200 cents)

1 13¢ + 22¢ + _____¢ = $1

2 33¢ + _____¢ + _____¢ = $1

3 _____¢ + _____¢ + _____¢ = $1

4 _____¢ + 75¢ + 64¢ = $2

5 _____¢ + 92¢ + _____¢ = $2

6 _____¢ + _____¢ + _____¢ = $2

NOTE

Students solve addition problems involving money.
MWI Adding More Than Two Numbers

NAME

DATE

Playing Array Games

Let's play *Count and Compare* together.

I have the following items:
○ A copy of the game directions
○ A list of "Facts I Know" and a list of "Facts I'm Working On"
○ My Array Cards

Let's play *Factor Pairs* together.

I have the following items:
○ A copy of the game directions
○ My Array Cards

Here are some of my Array Cards that we will be playing with.

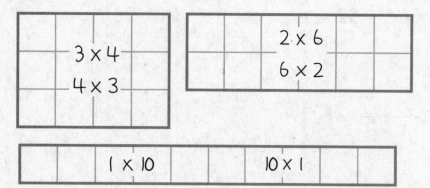

NOTE

The new game *Count and Compare* is designed to help your child learn multiplication facts. As you play with your child, ask questions about how he or she is figuring out the number of squares on each Array Card. Also revisit the array game *Factor Pairs,* which you and your child have already played together.
MWI **Learning Multiplication Facts**

Division Stories

Solve each of the problems below and show
your solution clearly.

 There are 28 desks in the classroom.
The teacher puts them in groups of 4.
How many groups of desks are in
the classroom?

 Three friends are given a pack of trading
cards to share equally. The pack contains
18 cards. How many cards should each
person get?

Division Stories

Solve each of the problems below and show
your solution clearly.

3 Becky has 30 flowers.
She wants to put them in bouquets of
5 flowers each.
How many bouquets will Becky be able
to make?

4 Seven children are building toy cars.
They have 28 toy wheels to share equally.
How many toy wheels will each child get?

NAME   DATE

Representing Division

Draw a picture or write an equation to represent each problem. Solve the problems any way you choose. Show your work.

 There are 42 players in a volleyball league.
Each team in the league has 7 players.
How many teams are in the league?

 A group of friends is sharing 18 slices of pizza equally.
Each friend eats 2 slices of pizza.
How many friends are there?

 Jessica bought 8 packages of hot dog buns.
She has 64 hot dog buns in all.
How many buns are in each package?

NOTE

Students solve division problems.
MWI **Solving Division Problems**

Story Problems

Solve each problem and show how you solved it.

 A robot has 4 hands. Each hand has 6 fingers. How many fingers does the robot have altogether?

 We made 20 muffins for the bake sale. We put the muffins in bags to sell. We put 4 muffins in each bag. How many bags of muffins did we have to sell?

 We bought 5 packs of yogurt cups. Each pack had 4 yogurt cups. How many yogurt cups did we buy?

Story Problems

4 Five children have one book of 35 movie tickets to share equally. Each movie costs one ticket. How many movies can each child see?

5 Before school my mother gave me a pack of 24 new pencils. When I get to school, I want to share them equally among my three friends and me. How many pencils will each of us get?

6 Benjamin drew a picture of 7 pentagons. Each pentagon has 5 sides. How many sides are there in all?

NAME _____ DATE _____

Packs, Students, Sides, and Frogs

Solve each problem and show your solution.

1 I bought 28 cups of yogurt. Each pack of yogurt has 4 cups. How many packs did I buy?

2 A teacher wants to put 25 students in 5 equal groups. How many students will be in each group?

3 I counted 24 sides on all of the triangles I drew. Each triangle has 3 sides. How many triangles did I draw?

4 There is a group of frogs in a pond. Each frog has 4 legs. I counted 24 legs. How many frogs are in the pond?

Ongoing Review

5 How many days are there in 6 weeks?

Ⓐ 42   Ⓑ 40   Ⓒ 36   Ⓓ 24

NOTE

Students solve division problems.
MWI Solving Division Problems

© Pearson Education 3

NAME   DATE

Multiplication and Division Stories

Draw a picture or write an equation to represent
each problem. Solve the problems any way you
choose. Show your work.

1. There are 36 students in Mr. Cahill's class.
His seating chart shows equal rows of 9 desks.
How many rows of desks did he make?

2. Melanie painted 5 petals on each of 8 flowers.
How many flower petals did she paint in all?

3. Rob's tennis coach brought 7 cans of balls to practice.
He has 21 tennis balls in all. How many balls are
in each can?

NOTE

Students solve multiplication and division story problems.
MWI Solving Division Problems

NAME   DATE

Multiply or Divide?

Solve each problem and show your solution.

 1 Zoë, Yuki, and Ivette have a bag of 30 pretzels.
They want to share them evenly.
How many pretzels should each student get?

2 Webster has 5 boxes of granola bars for his class.
Each box has 6 granola bars.
How many granola bars are there altogether?

 3 Latisha picks 24 flowers from her garden. She wants
to put the same number of flowers in each of 3 vases.
How many flowers should she put in each vase?

Ongoing Review

 4 If each letter is worth 5¢, how much money is the name
Maurice worth?

Ⓐ 30¢   Ⓑ 35¢   Ⓒ 40¢   Ⓓ 45¢

NOTE

Students solve multiplication and division problems.
MWI Solving Division Problems

NAME _____   DATE _____

Two-Part Problems

Solve these two-part problems and show your solutions.

1 Matthew has 30 boxes of raisins. There are 10 raisins in each box. He shares them equally with the children at his lunch table. There are 6 children altogether. How many raisins does each child get?

_____ boxes per child

_____ raisins per child

2 Jamal has 2 cats. Each cat has 4 kittens. Each kitten has 3 toys. How many toys do the kittens have altogether?

_____ kittens

_____ toys

Ongoing Review

3 There are 10 tables in the school cafeteria. Each table has 6 legs. If 4 more tables were added to the cafeteria, how many table legs would there be?

Ⓐ 34   Ⓑ 60   Ⓒ 64   Ⓓ 84

NOTE

Students solve multiplication and division problems.
MWI Solving Division Problems

Match Me Up!

 1 Match the picture to the problems. Then solve all of the problems.

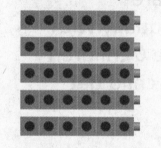

How many 4s in 20? _____

20 ÷ 4 = _____

5 groups of 4 are _____ altogether.

5 × 4 = _____

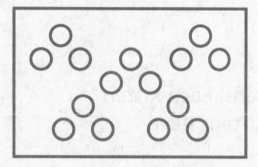

5 groups of 6 are _____ altogether.

5 × 6 = _____

How many 6s in 30? _____

30 ÷ 6 = _____

How many 3s in 15? _____

15 ÷ 3 = _____

5 groups of 3 are _____ altogether.

5 × 3 = _____

Ongoing Review

2 I counted 30 fingers around the table. How many people with 5 fingers on each hand were at the table?

Ⓐ 25   Ⓑ 10   Ⓒ 6   Ⓓ 3

NOTE

Students solve problems that involve relating multiplication and division.
MWI Relating Multiplication and Division

Graphs and
Line Plots

Graphs and
Line Plots

What Did You Find Out About Ms. Cutter's Grade 3 Class?

1 What is your question about where Ms. Cutter's students like to eat?

_____

_____

_____

_____

_____

2 List three things you found out from the data.

a. _____

_____

_____

b. _____

_____

_____

c. _____

_____

_____

NAME _____ DATE _____

What's the Missing Factor?

Solve the following sets of related problems.
Think about how to use one problem to solve
the next one.

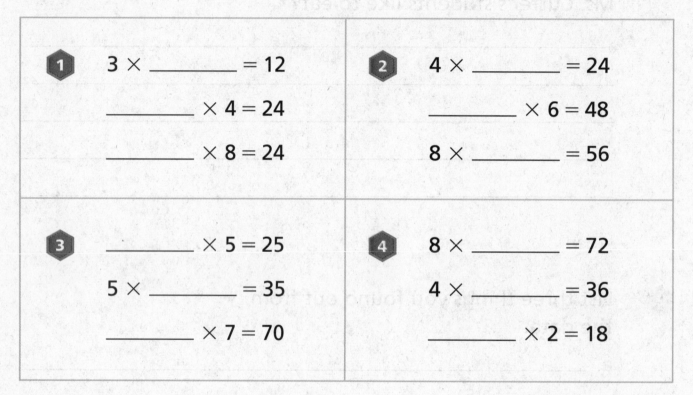

1 $3 \times \underline{\hspace{1.5cm}} = 12$

$\underline{\hspace{1.5cm}} \times 4 = 24$

$\underline{\hspace{1.5cm}} \times 8 = 24$

2 $4 \times \underline{\hspace{1.5cm}} = 24$

$\underline{\hspace{1.5cm}} \times 6 = 48$

$8 \times \underline{\hspace{1.5cm}} = 56$

3 $\underline{\hspace{1.5cm}} \times 5 = 25$

$5 \times \underline{\hspace{1.5cm}} = 35$

$\underline{\hspace{1.5cm}} \times 7 = 70$

4 $8 \times \underline{\hspace{1.5cm}} = 72$

$4 \times \underline{\hspace{1.5cm}} = 36$

$\underline{\hspace{1.5cm}} \times 2 = 18$

NOTE

Students solve missing factor problems.
MWI Related Multiplication Problems

© Pearson Education 3

About the Mathematics in This Unit

Dear Family,

Our class is starting a new mathematics unit about data called *Graphs and Line Plots*. During this unit, students collect, represent, describe, and interpret data.

Throughout the unit, students work toward these goals:

Benchmarks/Goals	Examples
Organize, represent, and describe categorical data, choosing categories that help make sense of the data.	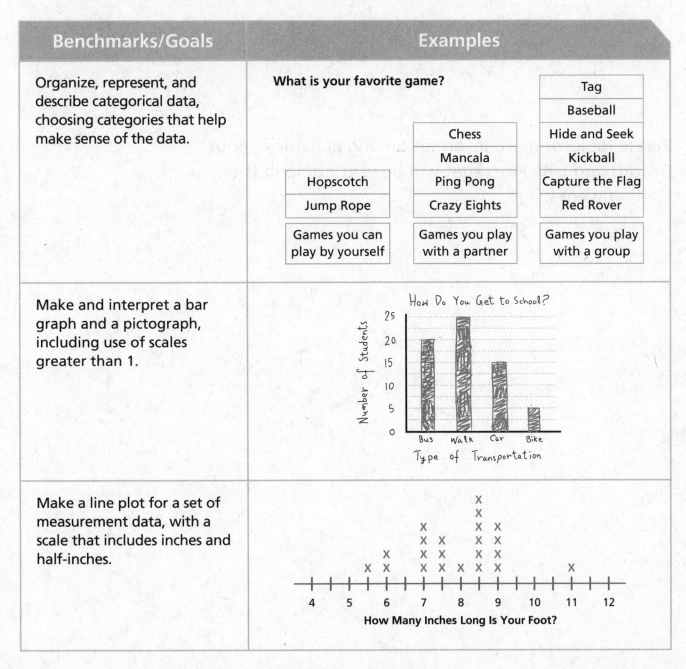
Make and interpret a bar graph and a pictograph, including use of scales greater than 1.	
Make a line plot for a set of measurement data, with a scale that includes inches and half-inches.	

About the Mathematics in This Unit

Benchmarks/Goals	Examples
Describe and summarize a set of data, describing concentrations of data and what those concentrations mean in terms of the situation the data represent.	More than half of the students in the class have feet measuring longer than 8 inches. Three students have feet that measure less than 7 inches long.
Generate measurement data by measuring lengths to the half-inch.	

Please look for more information and activities about *Graphs and Line Plots* that will be sent home in the coming weeks.

NAME

DATE

Adding 10s and 100s

Solve the following sets of related problems.
Think about how to use one problem to solve the
next one.

1   275 + 20 = _____

275 + 30 = _____

275 + 40 = _____

2   235 + 100 = _____

235 + 120 = _____

235 + 130 = _____

3   120 + 30 = _____

120 + 130 = _____

130 + 130 = _____

4   264 + 50 = _____

264 + 100 = _____

264 + 130 = _____

5   208 + 40 = _____

228 + 40 = _____

228 + 80 = _____

6   144 + 130 = _____

244 + 130 = _____

244 + 150 = _____

NOTE

Students practice adding multiples of 10 or 100 to 3-digit numbers.
MWI **Adding and Subtracting Tens and Hundreds**

NAME _____ DATE _____

Popular Pets

Here are data from Mr. Garcia's Grade 3 class about the pets that students have at home.

dog	cat	hamster	dog	lizard	cat
hamster	fish	bird	dog	fish	hamster
cat	bird	cat	cat	lizard	dog
dog	fish	dog	bird	hamster	dog

1 On a separate sheet of paper, organize the data above in a way that makes sense to you.

2 What can you say about the pets that students in Mr. Garcia's class have?

NOTE

Students organize data and list what they know from the data.
MWI Categorical Data

NAME

DATE

Related Activities to Try at Home

Dear Family,

The activities below are related to the mathematics in the data unit *Graphs and Line Plots*. You can use the activities to enrich your child's mathematical learning experience.

Guess My Rule During this unit, students collect data and learn about how to sort and classify these data. One way to build on this work is to play a guessing game about attributes and categories. One player lists things that belong to a category, and other players try to guess the category. For example, if the secret category is "things that are green," the person may say "grass, inchworms, dollar bills . . ."

You can also play *Guess My Rule* by gradually sorting a collection of 15 to 20 items (such as objects from the kitchen) into two groups. In one group, have objects that fit the rule, and in the other, have objects that do not fit the rule. A rule might be "is made of metal" or "is red." Start with just a few objects. As you continue to put objects into each group, your child tries to guess your rule.

Investigate a Topic Think of a question you want to answer about something in your house or your neighborhood. Collect data that will give you some information about your question. One investigation might be "How many times a day does our family use water?"

Related Activities to Try at Home

Together with your child, plan your data collection method. Make predictions about what you will find out. After you have collected your data, take some time to look closely at it. Does anything surprise you about the data you have collected? Do the data communicate any useful or interesting information about water use in your family? Your child may want to create some sort of representation of the data. Other questions you might investigate include "How much do we watch television?" or "Do cars stop at the stop sign at the end of our block?"

Data in the Media Look for examples of graphs in newspapers and magazines. Talk with your child about what these graphs represent. What do these graphs communicate? Discuss what choices the graph maker made and why the graph maker might have made these choices. What other choices might you make if you were creating a graph that represented these data?

NAME _____ DATE _____

What Is the Rule?

How do the things in the first group go together? Write the rule.

1

Fits the rule	Does **not** fit the rule

Rule: _____

2

Fits the rule	Does **not** fit the rule

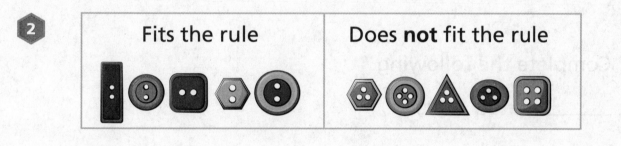

Rule: _____

3

Fits the rule		Does **not** fit the rule	
Guppy	Octopus	Giraffe	Chicken
Shark	Starfish	Dog	Mouse

Rule: _____

What are some other things that will fit the rule?

_____

NOTE

Students determine the rule by which objects have been sorted.
MWI **Categorical Data**

NAME   DATE

Hundred Pairs

1 Draw lines. Connect the pairs of numbers that make 100.

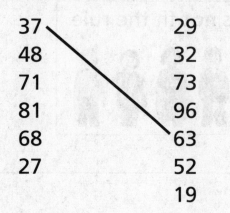

37	29
48	32
71	73
81	96
68	63
27	52
	19

2 Complete the following.

_____ + 55 = 100

15 + _____ = 100

30 + _____ = 100

_____ + 45 = 100

3 Find other pairs of numbers that make 100.

_____ + _____ = 100   _____ + _____ = 100

_____ + _____ = 100   _____ + _____ = 100

NOTE

Students practice finding combinations of 2-digit numbers that add up to 100.
MWI Tools to Represent Addition Problems

How Do You Get to School?

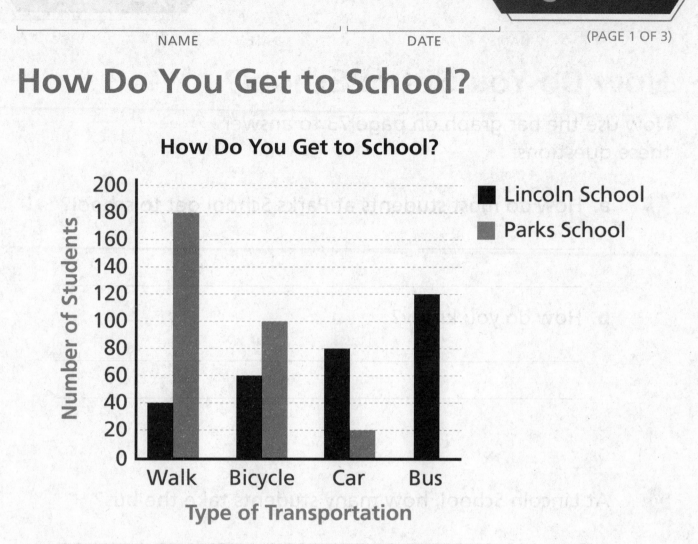

How Do You Get to School?

Look at the bar graph above. Write at least
3 things you can tell from looking at this graph.

1 _____

_____

2 _____

_____

3 _____

_____

How Do You Get to School?

Now use the bar graph on page 73 to answer
these questions:

4   **a.** How do most students at Parks School get to school?

_____

_____

b. How do you know?

_____

_____

5   At Lincoln School, how many students take the bus?

_____

6   **a.** How many students at Parks School do **NOT** walk to
school?

_____

b. How do you know?

_____

_____

How Do You Get to School?

 7 How many more students ride a bicycle to Parks School than ride a bicycle to Lincoln School?

_____

8 How many fewer students travel by car to Parks School than travel by car to Lincoln School?

_____

9 Compare how students travel to school at Lincoln School and Parks School. Are the ways the same or different? What might be some reasons for the similarities or differences?

_____

_____

_____

_____

NAME

DATE

How Many More to 200?

Solve the following problems and show your solutions on the number lines provided.

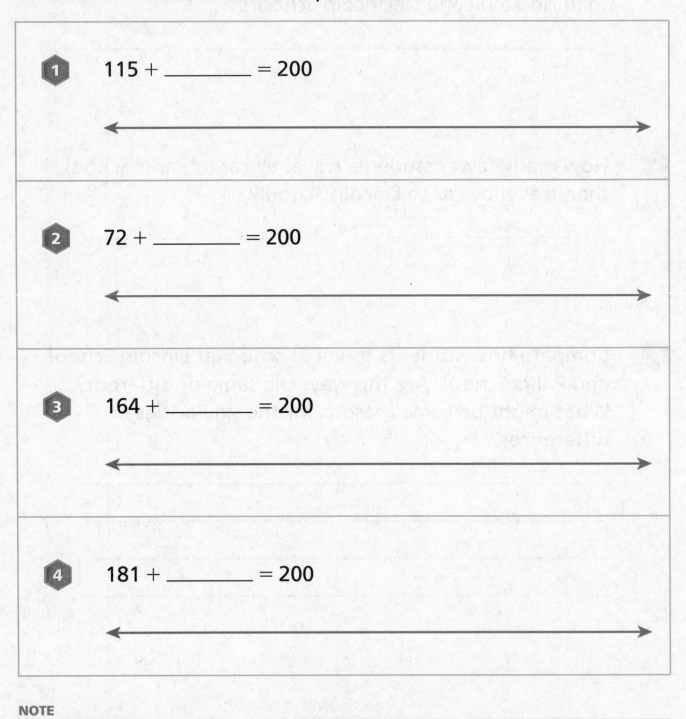

1. 115 + _____ = 200

2. 72 + _____ = 200

3. 164 + _____ = 200

4. 181 + _____ = 200

NOTE

Students practice finding combinations of 2-digit numbers that add up to 200.
MWI **Tools to Represent Addition Problems**

NAME _____ DATE _____

What Is Your Favorite Season?

Use the bar graph to answer the questions below.

What Is Your Favorite Season?

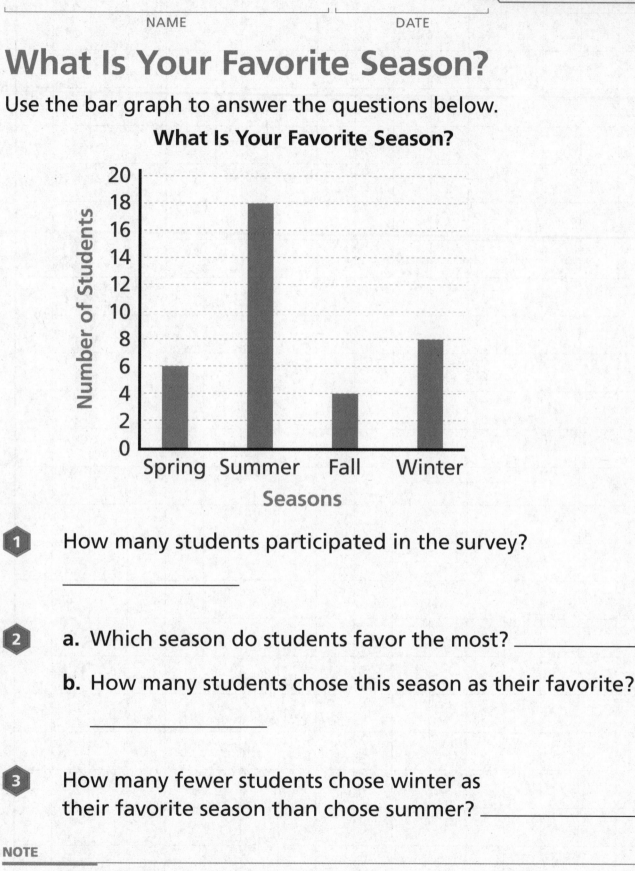

1 How many students participated in the survey?

_____

2 **a.** Which season do students favor the most? _____

b. How many students chose this season as their favorite?

_____

3 How many fewer students chose winter as their favorite season than chose summer? _____

NOTE _____

Students read and interpret data from a bar graph.
MWI **Bar Graphs**

Favorite Seasons

A class of 2nd graders took a survey of students at their school about their favorite season. These were the responses:

Summer	60	Spring	25	Fall	10	Winter	20

Make a bar graph of these data. Each square on the graph should represent more than 1. Then answer the following questions using your bar graph.

 1 How many students participated in the survey?

_____

2 **a.** Which season is the favorite?

_____

b. How many students chose this season as their favorite?

_____

3 Summer and spring are the warmer seasons. Winter and fall are the colder seasons. Did more students choose warmer seasons or colder seasons? How many more?

_____

4 How many more votes did summer get than the other three seasons put together?

_____

Making and Interpreting Pictographs

Use the data to make a pictograph. Make each picture represent more than 1.

Favorite Sports Chosen by Students	
Sport Chosen	**Number of Students**
Baseball	8
Basketball	4
Football	12
Soccer	6

Title:	

Key: Each _____ = _____

Making and Interpreting Pictographs

Use your pictograph to answer the questions.

1 Which sport was chosen by the greatest number of students?

2 Which sport was chosen by the least number of students?

3 How many more students chose football than basketball?

4 Suppose you added another sport to your graph. How many pictures would you draw if you wanted to show that 10 students chose hockey?

NAME

DATE

Pictographs

The pictograph shows the numbers of 5 different paper airplane types made by students in Mr. Miller's class. Use the pictograph to answer the questions.

Paper Airplanes Made by Students	
Dart	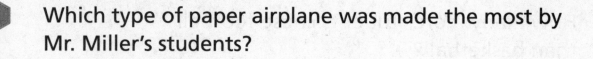
Delta Wing	
Fighter	
Glider	
Flying Wing	

Each = 2 planes

1 Which type of paper airplane was made the most by Mr. Miller's students?

2 How many paper airplanes of this type were made?

3 How many more Fighters were made than Darts?

4 Students made 4 fewer Flying Wings than what other type of plane?

NOTE

Students interpret a pictograph.
MWI **Pictographs**

© Pearson Education 3

What Is Your Favorite Mealtime?

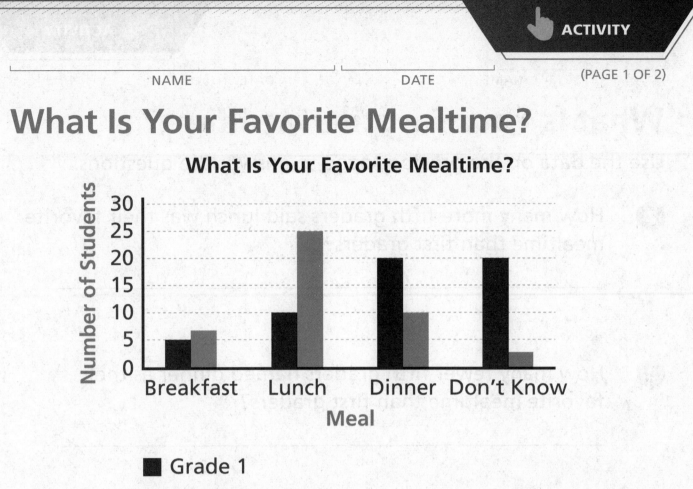

What Is Your Favorite Mealtime?

- ■ Grade 1
- ■ Grade 5

1 Compare the responses of the first graders and the fifth graders. How are they the same or different?

_____

_____

_____

© Pearson Education 3

What Is Your Favorite Mealtime?

Use the data on the previous page to answer the questions.

 2 How many more fifth graders said lunch was their favorite mealtime than first graders?

_____

 3 How many fewer fifth graders named dinner as their favorite mealtime than first graders?

_____

4 Write three other things you can tell from looking at the graph.

a. _____

_____

_____

b. _____

_____

_____

c. _____

_____

_____

What is Your Favorite Fruit?

Oranges	8
Strawberries	25
Apples	15
Bananas	32

Make a bar graph of the data above. Make each square represent more than 1.

What Color Are Your Eyes?

Some first graders took a survey of other students about the color of their eyes. These were their responses:

Brown   28
Blue   10
Green   5

Make a pictograph of the data. Make each picture represent more than 1.

NAME

DATE

Subtracting 10s and 100s

Solve the following sets of related problems. Think about how to use one problem to solve the next.

1 103 − 70 = _____

123 − 70 = _____

173 − 70 = _____

2 200 − 60 = _____

212 − 60 = _____

222 − 60 = _____

3 300 − 90 = _____

250 − 90 = _____

225 − 90 = _____

4 134 − 40 = _____

144 − 40 = _____

144 − 60 = _____

5 167 − 50 = _____

167 − 100 = _____

267 − 100 = _____

6 469 − 200 = _____

479 − 200 = _____

479 − 300 = _____

NOTE

Students practice subtracting multiples of 10 from 3 digit numbers.

MW1 Adding and Subtracting Tens and Hundreds

NAME

DATE

Favorite Sports

Use the bar graph to answer the questions below.

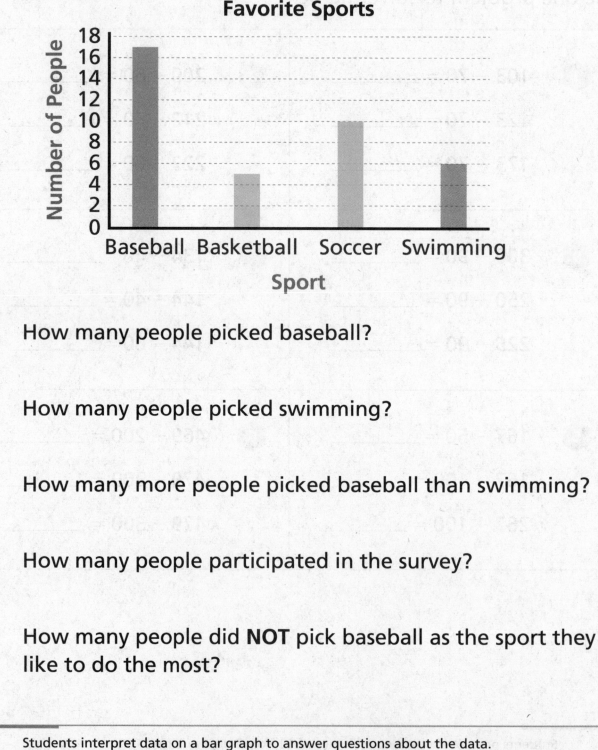

Favorite Sports

1 How many people picked baseball?

2 How many people picked swimming?

3 How many more people picked baseball than swimming?

4 How many people participated in the survey?

5 How many people did **NOT** pick baseball as the sport they like to do the most?

NOTE

Students interpret data on a bar graph to answer questions about the data.
MWI Describing and Summarizing Data

NAME   DATE

Displaying Data

1   How could you group these students?
Make a pictograph to represent your data.

Each _____ = _____ students.

2   How many people are in your first category?

_____

_____

3   How many people are in your second category?

_____

_____

4   Which category has more people? How many more people?

_____

_____

NOTE

Students group a given set of data, and answer questions about it.
MWI **Categorical Data**

NAME

DATE

Story Problems

For each problem, write an equation, solve the problem, and show your solution.

1 Deondra has 72 collectible figurines.
She displays them equally on 9 shelves.
How many figurines are displayed on each shelf?

2 Greg made 3 batches of pancakes for breakfast.
There are 6 pancakes in each batch.
How many pancakes did Greg make in all?

3 Liza bought 35 stickers to decorate her school folders.
She put an equal number of stickers on each of 5 folders.
How many stickers did she put on each folder?

NOTE

Students solve multiplication and division story problems.
MWI Solving Division Problems

NAME _____   DATE _____

Addition Practice

Solve the following sets of related problems.
Think about how to use one problem to solve the next.

1 135 + 50 = _____

155 + 50 = _____

135 + 150 = _____

2 305 + 70 = _____

335 + 70 = _____

435 + 70 = _____

3 220 + 30 = _____

220 + 130 = _____

250 + 130 = _____

4 161 + 50 = _____

261 + 60 = _____

361 + 60 = _____

5 318 + 200 = _____

368 + 200 = _____

218 + 200 = _____

6 264 + 200 = _____

264 + 250 = _____

274 + 250 = _____

NOTE

Students practice adding multiples of 10 or 100 to 3 digit numbers.
MWI **Adding and Subtracting Tens and Hundreds**

NAME _____ DATE _____

Familiar Facts

Solve the following sets of related problems. Think about how to use one problem to solve the next one.

1

$2 \times 7 =$ _____

$7 \times 2 =$ _____

$14 \div 7 =$ _____

$14 \div$ _____ $= 7$

2

$3 \times$ _____ $= 15$

_____ $\times 3 = 15$

$15 \div$ _____ $= 3$

$15 \div 3 =$ _____

3

_____ $\times 8 = 32$

$8 \times 4 =$ _____

_____ $\div 4 = 8$

$32 \div$ _____ $= 4$

4

$6 \times$ _____ $= 60$

$10 \times$ _____ $= 30$

$60 \div$ _____ $= 6$

$30 \div 10 =$ _____

NOTE

Students practice solving multiplication and division problems.

MWI **Relating Multiplication and Division**

How Many Years in This School?

Ms. G's Grade 5 class in King School took a survey about how many years they have been in their school. Here is the list of the students in the class and how many years each student has been in the school.

Name	Years	Name	Years	Name	Years	Name	Years
Jane	1	Greg	2	Kari	5	Frank	3
Elisa	6	Phil	1	Holly	2	Keith	1
Rob	4	Linnea	5	Sam	1	Alice	2
Ann	2	Marie	4	Pete	1	Susan	6
Steve	2	Mel	5	Jeff	3	David	4
Deb	1	Jesse	2	Liza	2		

1 Draw a line plot of the data in the space below or on grid paper.

How Many Years in This School?

2 What can you say about the number of years the students in Ms. G's class have been in King School? Write at least 3 things you can say about the data.

a. _____

_____

_____

_____

b. _____

_____

_____

_____

c. _____

_____

_____

_____

More Addition Practice

Solve the following sets of related problems. Think about how to use one problem to solve the next.

1 $345 + 50 =$ _____

$345 + 60 =$ _____

$325 + 60 =$ _____

2 $240 + 150 =$ _____

$250 + 150 =$ _____

$350 + 150 =$ _____

3 $110 + 250 =$ _____

$120 + 250 =$ _____

$120 + 350 =$ _____

4 $167 + 300 =$ _____

$167 + 200 =$ _____

$267 + 100 =$ _____

5 $218 + 300 =$ _____

$218 + 250 =$ _____

$268 + 250 =$ _____

6 $274 + 100 =$ _____

$274 + 150 =$ _____

$274 + 200 =$ _____

NOTE

Students practice adding multiples of 10 or 100 to 3-digit numbers.
MWI Adding and Subtracting Tens and Hundreds

NAME _____ DATE _____

Multiplication and Division Story Problems

In 1 and 2, write an equation that represents each story problem. Then solve each problem and show your solution.

1 There are 2 flowers in each of 8 flower pots. How many flowers are there in all?

2 Kenji's dad ran 70 miles in 10 days. He ran the same distance each day. How many miles did Kenji's dad run each day?

In 3 and 4, write a math story problem for each expression. Then solve each problem and show your solution.

3 4 × 8

4 81 ÷ 9

NOTE

Students practice solving and writing multiplication and division story problems.
 Solving Multiplication Problems

Measuring

1 Foot Length (to the nearest half inch)

a. How long is your foot?

_____

b. Is your foot a foot long, or is it shorter or longer than a foot?

_____

2 Pattern Block Distance (to the nearest half inch or feet and nearest half inch) How far did you blow the pattern block?

_____

3 Classroom Length (in feet and inches)

a. First time: _____

b. Second time: _____

4 Jump Distance (in feet and inches and in inches) How far did you jump?

a. _____ feet and _____ inches

b. _____ inches

NAME _____ DATE _____

Foot Findings

Colin measured the length of every teacher's foot to the nearest half inch. Here are the data:

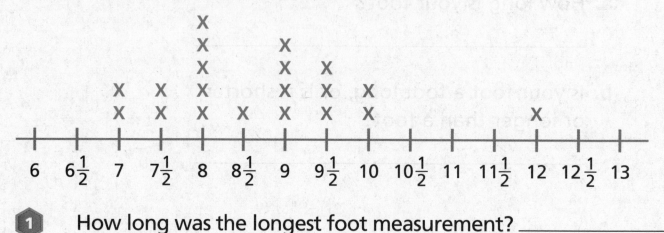

1 How long was the longest foot measurement? _____

2 What was the typical length for all?

_____

_____

3 How did you determine the typical length for all feet measured?

4 Describe 2 things you notice about the data, including where data are spread out or concentrated, where there are few data, and what the range is.

NOTE

Students analyze data on a line plot.
MWI **Organizing and Representing Data**

UNIT 2 | 98 | SESSION 2.2   © Pearson Education 3

Reach for the Sky!

The students in Mr. Burke's class used inches to measure how high they could reach without standing on their tiptoes. Here are their data:

Keisha	59	Nicholas	60	Gina	$63\frac{1}{2}$	Kim	63
Pilar	60	Kelley	$61\frac{1}{2}$	Kenji	61	Jung	62
Benjamin	63	Jane	61	Oscar	60	Adam	64
Denzel	62	Nancy	$63\frac{1}{2}$	Inez	62	Keith	$61\frac{1}{2}$

1   Use the data to make a line plot.

2   The students' reaches ranged from _____ to _____ inches.

NOTE

Students represent and describe a set of data.
MWI Organizing and Representing Data

Reach for the Sky!

3 Describe 2 things you notice about the data, including where data are spread out or are concentrated, where there are few data, and whether there are outliers.

_____

_____

_____

_____

_____

Ongoing Review

4 Solve the equation. Choose the missing value.

$$49 \div \underline{\hspace{2cm}} = 7$$

Ⓐ 9   Ⓑ 8   Ⓒ 7   Ⓓ 6

NAME

DATE

Giant Steps

This data table shows how many giant steps students in Room 222 took to walk the length of their classroom. On a separate sheet of paper, create a line plot to represent the data.

14	11	13	13	18	11	14	15	14	13
13	15	13	14	14	15	15	12	14	

1 How many students participated in the survey? _____

2 What number of giant steps were taken by more students than any other number of steps? _____

3 What were the fewest giant steps taken to walk the length of the classroom? _____

4 What were the most giant steps taken to walk the length of the classroom? _____

Ongoing Review

5 Which of the following accurately describes the difference between the most giant steps taken and the fewest giant steps taken?

Ⓐ 2 steps   Ⓑ 5 steps   Ⓒ 7 steps   Ⓓ 10 steps

NOTE

Students describe data on a line plot.
MWI **Describing and Summarizing Data**

NAME

DATE

Measurement of Rabbits

A scientist measured the length of some rabbits to the nearest half inch. Here are the data she gathered:

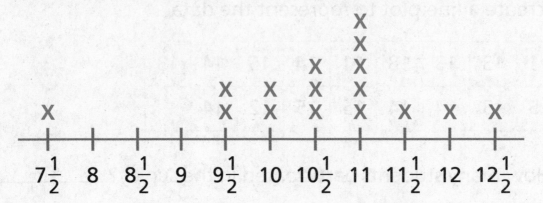

1 What was the length of the longest rabbit?

2 What was the typical length of the rabbits?

3 Is there an outlier in the line plot data? If so, what is it?

4 Describe two things you notice about the data, including where data are spread out or concentrated, where there are few data, and what the range is.

NOTE

Students describe data represented in a line plot.
MWI **Describing and Summarizing Data**

Feet and Inches

In a Grade 3 class, some students were playing Blowing a Pattern Block. They measured how far each student blew the block.

Benjamin: 1 ruler and 3 more inches
Jung: 1 ruler and $6\frac{1}{2}$ more inches
Chris: 2 rulers
Elena: 1 ruler and $\frac{1}{2}$ a ruler

1 Use rulers to show how far each student blew the pattern block. How far did each block go in inches, to the nearest $\frac{1}{2}$ inch? How far did each block go in feet and inches?

How far did the students blow the pattern block?

	Inches	Feet and Inches
Benjamin		
Jung		
Chris		
Elena		

Feet and Inches

Later, the same students were jumping with both feet. They measured their jumps by putting rulers end to end.

Here is how long the jumps were:

Benjamin: 4 rulers and $2\frac{1}{2}$ more inches
Jung: 3 rulers and 4 more inches
Chris: 5 rulers
Elena: 4 rulers and 11 more inches

2 Use rulers to show how far each student jumped. How far did each student jump in inches? How far did each student jump in feet and inches?

How far did the students jump?

	Inches	Feet and Inches
Benjamin		
Jung		
Chris		
Elena		

Today's Number

Today's Number is 157.

Write 3 equations that equal 157. You must do the following:

- Use both addition and subtraction in each equation.

- Use 2 multiples of 10 in each equation.

Equation 1: _____

Equation 2: _____

Equation 3: _____

NAME _____ DATE _____

More Multiplication and Division Problems

Solve the following problems and show how
you solved them.

1 A league has 30 basketball players. Each
team has 5 players. How many teams are
in the league?

2 Jane has 6 bags of apples. Each bag has
8 apples. How many apples does Jane have?

3 There are 24 students in Mr. Smith's class.
He splits the class into groups of 4. How
many groups are there?

4 Edwin has 9 bunches of bananas. Each
bunch has 5 bananas on it. How many
bananas does Edwin have?

NOTE

Students solve multiplication and division word problems.
MWI Solving Multiplication Problems; Solving Division Problems

How Far Can a Grade 3 Student Blow a Pattern Block?

1   On another sheet of paper, make a line plot to show the data from your class.

2   Write at least 3 things you notice about the data. (If you have more to say, you can write more ideas on a blank sheet of paper.)

   a. _____

      _____

      _____

   b. _____

      _____

      _____

   c. _____

      _____

      _____

3   If someone asked you, "How far can a Grade 3 student blow a pattern block?" what would you say, according to the data?

NAME   DATE

Making Graphs

The table below shows the number of books read by students in a Grade 3 class in one month.

Name	Number of Books Read	Name	Number of Books Read
Ines	8	Chris	7
Philip	9	Gina	9
Jane	18	Adam	8
Oscar	11	Murphy	9
Edwin	7	Kenji	10
Jung	8	Bridget	6
Nancy	9	Zhang	6
Gil	4	Elena	22
Kim	9	Keisha	12

Make a line plot using the data from the table.

NOTE

Students are able to use data to create a line plot and a bar graph.
MWI **Organizing and Representing Data**

NAME

DATE

Missing Factors and Division Facts

Solve the following sets of related problems. Think about how to use one problem to solve the next one.

1 $2 \times \underline{\hspace{2cm}} = 12$

$12 \div 2 = \underline{\hspace{2cm}}$

$\underline{\hspace{2cm}} \times 4 = 12$

$12 \div \underline{\hspace{2cm}} = 4$

2 $4 \times \underline{\hspace{2cm}} = 20$

$20 \div 4 = \underline{\hspace{2cm}}$

$\underline{\hspace{2cm}} \times 2 = 20$

$20 \div \underline{\hspace{2cm}} = 2$

3 $6 \times \underline{\hspace{2cm}} = 42$

$42 \div 6 = \underline{\hspace{2cm}}$

$\underline{\hspace{2cm}} \times 8 = 48$

$48 \div 8 = \underline{\hspace{2cm}}$

4 $7 \times \underline{\hspace{2cm}} = 21$

$21 \div 7 = \underline{\hspace{2cm}}$

$\underline{\hspace{2cm}} \times 7 = 63$

$63 \div 7 = \underline{\hspace{2cm}}$

5 $9 \times \underline{\hspace{2cm}} = 36$

$36 \div 9 = \underline{\hspace{2cm}}$

$\underline{\hspace{2cm}} \times 6 = 36$

$36 \div \underline{\hspace{2cm}} = 6$

6 $\underline{\hspace{2cm}} \times 3 = 15$

$15 \div 3 = \underline{\hspace{2cm}}$

$8 \times \underline{\hspace{2cm}} = 24$

$24 \div \underline{\hspace{2cm}} = 8$

NOTE

Students use known multiplication facts to solve division problems.

MW1 Relating Multiplication and Division

Travel Stories and Collections

Travel Stories and
Collections

NAME

DATE

Pictograph Practice

1 Use the information in the data table to complete the pictograph.

Rory's Sports Card Collections	
Sport	**Number of Cards**
Baseball	75
Football	40
Basketball	65
Hockey	50
Soccer	35

Title:	

Key: Each _____ = _____

Ongoing Review

2 Which pair of card collections has more cards than the sum of the Baseball and Hockey collections? Use the data table and your pictograph to solve.

Ⓐ Baseball and Football   Ⓒ Football and Basketball

Ⓑ Hockey and Soccer   Ⓓ Baseball and Basketball

NOTE

Students create a pictograph from given data.
MWI Pictographs

NAME   DATE

About the Mathematics in This Unit

Dear Family,

Our class is starting a new mathematics unit about addition and subtraction called *Travel Stories and Collections*. In this unit, students practice and refine addition and subtraction strategies and solve different types of subtraction problems. They work on understanding the place value of 3-digit numbers and learn about the size of the number 1,000.

Throughout the unit, students work toward the following goals:

Benchmarks/Goals	Examples
Use knowledge of place value to read, write, sequence, and round numbers up to 1,000.	Put the following numbers in order on the number line below. Then circle the number you would round to 300 when rounding to the nearest 100. 423 234 432 342
Solve addition problems with 3-digit numbers (up to 400) by using strategies that involve breaking numbers apart, either by place value or by adding one number in parts.	**Solve:** 286 $+138$ 286 $+138$ 300 110 $+\ 14$ 424 $200 + 100 = 300$ $80 + 30 = 110$ $6 + 8 = \ 14$ $300 + 110 + 14 = 424$
Solve subtraction problems with 2- and 3-digit numbers (up to 300) by using strategies that involve either subtracting one number in parts or finding the difference by adding up or subtracting back.	**Solve:** 148 $-\ 62$ $148 -\ \ 2 = 146$ $146 - 40 = 106$ $106 - 20 = \ 86$

About the Mathematics in This Unit

This unit is the first of two units that focus on addition, subtraction, and the number system in Grade 3. Later this year, students will continue to work on developing accurate and efficient strategies for both addition and subtraction. In our math class, students spend time discussing problems in depth and are asked to share their reasoning and solutions. It is important that children accurately and efficiently solve math problems in ways that make sense to them. At home, encourage your child to explain his or her math thinking to you. Please look for more information and activities from Unit 3 that will be sent home in the coming weeks.

Sticker Station Problems

Write an equation that represents the problem.
Then solve the problem, and show your work.

1 Maria had 146 stickers. She went to the
Sticker Station and bought 3 more strips
of 10 and 2 singles. How many stickers
does Maria have now?

2 Ari had 163 sea-animal stickers. His
mother gave him 26 more sea-animal
stickers. How many sea-animal stickers
does he have now?

3 Vanessa went to Sticker Station and
bought 6 strips of 10 and 3 single star
stickers, and 1 sheet of 100, 5 strips of 10,
and 9 single moon stickers. How many
stickers did Vanessa buy in all?

Sticker Station Problems

4 Seth went to Sticker Station. He bought
1 sheet of 100, 4 strips of 10, and 6 single
soccer stickers, and he bought 8 strips of
10 and 3 single animal stickers. How many
stickers did Seth buy?

5 Diana bought 28 balloon stickers at the
Sticker Station. Her sister gave her
223 more. How many does she have now?

6 Tanji bought 365 flower stickers at the
Sticker Station. Her sister gave her
51 more. How many does she have now?

NAME

DATE

Problems for *Capture 5*

Ava and Leo are playing *Capture 5.*

1 Ava's game piece is on 36. She wants to capture a chip that is on 72.

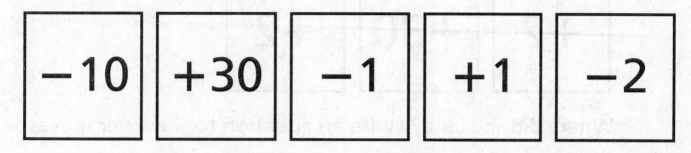

Can she do it with these Change Cards? If so, how? If not, explain why not.

2 Leo's game piece is on 50. There are three chips left on 6, 39, and 73.

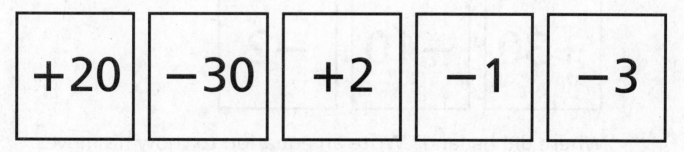

Can Leo capture any of the chips with these Change Cards? If so, how? If not, explain why not.

NOTE

Students solve problems that involve adding and subtracting multiples of 10.
MWI Adding and Subtracting Tens and Hundreds

© Pearson Education 3

NAME

DATE

Writing Equations for *Capture 5*

1 Michelle's game piece was on 58. She used these cards to capture a chip:

| +2 | +30 | +2 |

Where did she land? Write an equation to show her moves.

Equation: _____

2 Jamal's game piece was on 19. He used these cards to capture a chip:

| +30 | −10 | −2 |

Where did he land? Write an equation to show his moves.

Equation: _____

NOTE

This homework is based on a math game that students have been playing in which they practice adding and subtracting 10s and 1s and writing equations.
MWI Equations With Two Operations

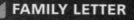
Related Activities to Try at Home

Dear Family,

The activities below are related to the mathematics in this addition and subtraction unit. You can use the activities to enrich your child's mathematical learning experience.

Collect 1,000 Together you and your child can collect 1,000 of the same small objects to see what a collection of exactly 1,000 objects (such as pebbles, bread tabs, gallon milk lids, or popsicle sticks) looks like. As you collect the objects, organize them in groups of 10 and groups of 100 to help you keep track of them. Before you begin, estimate how long you think it will take to collect 1,000 objects and how much space you think your objects will take up. As your collection grows, you might adjust your estimates on the basis of how long it has taken so far or how much space several hundred take up.

What Time Is It? In this and other units, students practice telling time during an activity called What Time Is It? Students learn to tell time first to the nearest 5 minutes (5:20) and then to the nearest minute (5:28) on both digital and analog clocks. They also identify intervals of time, such as the starting and ending time of an activity.

Related Activities to Try at Home

What Time Is It? (continued)

You can continue to help your child practice telling time by asking questions, such as the following, as they come up during your everyday activities:

- Look at the clock. What time is it now?
- We are going to have dinner in 45 minutes. What time will it be then?
- How many more minutes until Aunt Sara gets here at 5:00?
- We left the house at 8:10 and returned at 9:05. How long were we gone?
- If you started reading at 5:17 and read for 30 minutes, what time was it when you stopped?

How Many More Stickers to Get 100?

Solve each problem below, and record your strategy by using equations. If you used 100 grids, the 100 Chart, or the class number line, show how you used those tools.

 1 Misaki went to Sticker Station. She bought 28 animal stickers. How many more does she need to have 100 animal stickers?

2 Ryan bought 43 flower stickers at Sticker Station. How many more does he need to have 100 flower stickers?

How Many More Stickers to Get 100?

3 **a.** Ana went to Sticker Station on Tuesday and bought 37 airplane stickers. On Friday, she bought 42 more. How many does she have now?

b. How many more stickers does Ana need to have 100 airplane stickers?

4 **a.** Derek has 24 baseball stickers. He went to Sticker Station and bought 35 more baseball stickers. How many does he have now?

b. How many more stickers does Derek need to have 100 baseball stickers?

More Sticker Station Problems

Write an equation that represents the problem. Then solve the problem, and show your work.

1 Deondra has 284 baseball stickers. She has 73 basketball stickers. How many baseball and basketball stickers does she have?

2 On Monday, Arthur bought 2 sheets of 100, 3 strips of 10, and 7 single stickers. On Tuesday, he bought 6 strips of 10 and 9 single stickers. How many stickers did Arthur buy in all?

3 Kim has 145 insect stickers. Her friend gave her 81 more insect stickers. Now how many insect stickers does Kim have?

4 Zhang bought 2 sheets of 100, 2 strips of 10, and 2 single sea-animal stickers. He bought 9 strips of 10 and 8 single soccer stickers. How many stickers did he buy?

NAME

DATE

How Many More to 50?

Solve each problem, and show your work.

1 $14 +$ _____ $= 50$

2 $32 +$ _____ $= 50$

3 $8 +$ _____ $= 50$

4 $26 +$ _____ $= 50$

5 $41 +$ _____ $= 50$

6 $12 +$ _____ $= 50$

NOTE

Students practice finding combinations of numbers that equal 50.

MWI **Addition Strategies: Adding by Place; Adding One Number in Parts**

NAME   DATE

Stickers, Bottles, and Marbles

Write an equation that represents the problem.
Then solve the problem, and show your work.

1 Seth went to Sticker Station. He bought
3 strips of 10 and 6 single soccer stickers,
and he bought 8 strips of 10 and 3 single
animal stickers. How many stickers did
Seth buy?

2 Janelle collected bottles to bring to the
recycling center. She collected 64 bottles
on Saturday and 55 bottles on Sunday.
How many bottles did she bring to the
recycling center?

3 James had 67 marbles. He gave 30 of the
marbles to his sister. How many marbles
does he have now?

NOTE

These problems provide practice for adding and subtracting 2-digit numbers.
Ask your child to explain how he or she solved each problem.
MWI **Subtraction Strategies: Adding Up and Subtracting Back**

NAME

DATE

Sums That Equal 100

Solve these problems and show your work.

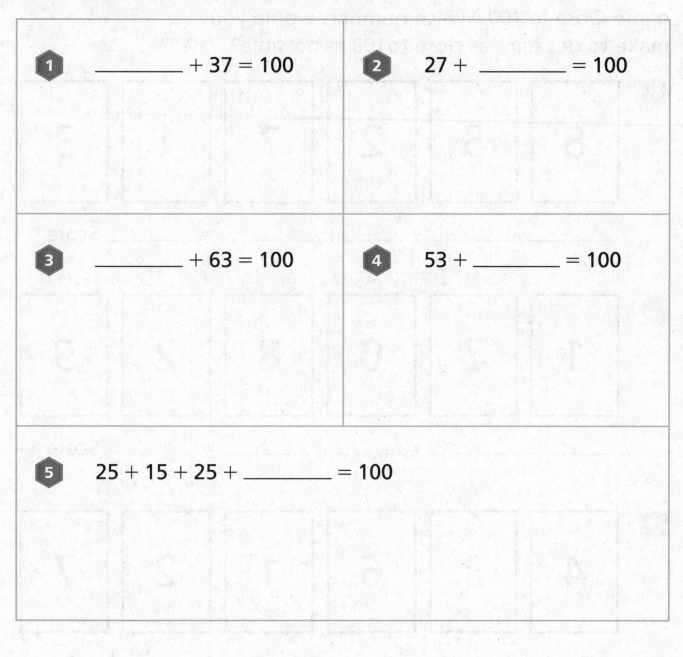

1 _____ + 37 = 100

2 27 + _____ = 100

3 _____ + 63 = 100

4 53 + _____ = 100

5 25 + 15 + 25 + _____ = 100

NOTE

Students practice finding sums that equal 100.
MWI Adding More Than Two Numbers

NAME _____ DATE _____

Problems for *Close to 100*

Suppose that you are dealt these hands in the game *Close to 100.* Which numbers would you make to get sums as close to 100 as possible?

1

8	5	2	7	1	3

_____ _____ + _____ _____ = _____ Score

2

1	7	0	8	2	9

_____ _____ + _____ _____ = _____ Score

3

4	3	6	1	2	7

_____ _____ + _____ _____ = _____ Score

NOTE

Students practice finding pairs of 2-digit numbers that add to 100. Ask your child to explain how he or she chose which cards to use.
MWI **Addition Strategies: Changing the Numbers**

137 Stickers

Show all of the ways you can think of to make the number 137 with stickers.

Sheets of 100	Strips of 10	Singles

137 Stickers

Show all of the ways you can think of to make the number 137 with stickers.

Sheets of 100	Strips of 10	Singles

NAME

DATE

Flag Stickers

1 Leslie bought 158 flag stickers. They come in sheets of 100, strips of 10, and singles. Sketch at least five different combinations for 158. Write an equation for each combination.

Ongoing Review

2 How many stickers are represented by this sketch?

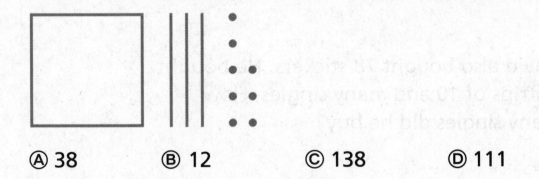

Ⓐ 38   Ⓑ 12   Ⓒ 138   Ⓓ 111

NOTE

Students practice making representations of numbers using 100s, 10s, and 1s.
MWI **Ones, Tens, and Hundreds**

© Pearson Education 3

NAME

DATE

Problems for 78 Stickers

Solve the problems below, and show your work.
Write an equation for each combination of
strips and singles.

 1 Emma bought 78 stickers at Sticker Station.
She bought 7 strips of 10 and some singles.
How many singles did she buy?

70 + _____ = 78

2 Kiara bought 78 stickers as well. She
bought 6 strips of 10 and some singles.
How many singles did she buy?

3 Joshua bought 78 stickers, too. He bought
4 strips of 10 and some singles. How many
singles did he buy?

4 David also bought 78 stickers. He bought
2 strips of 10 and many singles. How
many singles did he buy?

NOTE

Students practice making different combinations of 10s and 1s for a number.
MWI **Many Ways to Make 145**

NAME _____ DATE _____

Finding Numbers on the 1,000 Chart

1 Look at each set of numbers. Find the spaces on your 1,000 Chart where each number should be located. Then, write each number in the correct space.

Set A:	43	143	643	843
Set B:	378	358	328	318
Set C:	775	275	575	975
Set D:	813	833	853	873
Set E:	67	267	467	667
Set F:	227	257	277	297

2 Choose one set of numbers and explain how you found those numbers on your 1,000 Chart.

_____

_____

_____

_____

_____

NAME

DATE

Addition and the 700 Chart

Solve these problems. Fill in the sums on the 700 Chart.

1 616 + 50 = _____

2 613 + 60 = _____

3 688 + 10 = _____

4 611 + 20 = _____

5 602 + 40 = _____

6 664 + 20 = _____

7 608 + 20 = _____

8 609 + 50 = _____

9 600 + 10 = _____

601			604					609	
					616				
	622								630
				635					
641						647			
		653							
							668		
					676				680
	682								
			694			697			700

Ongoing Review

10 The sum of which expression does **NOT** belong on the 700 Chart?

Ⓐ 634 + 70   Ⓒ 684 + 10

Ⓑ 601 + 40   Ⓓ 617 + 80

NOTE

Students review the place value of 3-digit numbers as they add 10s to any number. They also find and write the sums on the 700 Chart.

MWI Tools to Represent Addition Problems

NAME   DATE

Collections: Smallest to Largest

1 Make a list of the Collection Card categories.

_____   _____

_____   _____

_____   _____

2 Choose two categories and pull out all of the cards in those categories. You will have 8 cards to put in order. Starting with the smallest number and moving to the largest, write the number of items in each collection in order.

Collection Categories: _____ and _____

Smallest   to   Largest

_____ _____ _____ _____ _____ _____ _____ _____

3 Find each of these numbers on your 1,000 Chart and write in any numbers that are not already there.

How Many 10s? Part 1

Solve the problems below. You may use your
1,000 Chart to help you.

 The students in Mr. Jackson's class are
collecting pennies. They decide to display
them in stacks of 10. How many stacks can
they make with 345 pennies? How many
single pennies will they have left?

Explain how you figured it out.

 The students in Ms. Kennedy's class are
collecting stamps from old letters. They are
displaying the stamps in rows of 10. How
many rows can they make with 428 stamps?

Explain how you figured it out.

How Many 10s? Part 1

3 The students in Ms. Vega's class are collecting pull tabs from juice cans. They are hanging them on a bulletin board in bags of 10. On Wednesday, they had 536 pull tabs. How many bags of 10 were on the board? How many single pull tabs were left over?

Explain how you figured it out.

4 On Friday, the students in Ms. Vega's class had 58 bags of pull tabs on their bulletin board and 7 single pull tabs on the counter. How many pull tabs did they have?

Explain how you figured it out.

NAME

DATE

Story Problems

Birds have 2 legs.
Dogs have 4 legs.
Ladybugs have 6 legs.

 There are 36 legs and they all belong to dogs. How many dogs are there?

 There are 48 legs and they all belong to ladybugs. How many ladybugs are there?

 There are 3 ladybugs, 7 dogs, and 10 birds. How many legs are there altogether?

NOTE

Students use multiplication and division to solve word problems.
MWI Solving Division Problems

NAME   DATE

More Problems for *Close to 100*

 Tom and Shanice are playing *Close to 100*.

Tom has these cards: Shanice has these cards:

| 3 | 6 | 4 | 9 | 2 | 7 | | 6 | 6 | 1 | 8 | 3 | 5 |

Find the 4 cards that will get each player as close to 100 as possible.

Tom	Shanice
___ + ___ = ___	___ + ___ = ___

2 Who is closer to 100? _____

3 Choose either Tom's or Shanice's hand. Explain how you chose which cards to use to get as close to 100 as possible.

NOTE

Students practice finding pairs of 2-digit numbers that add as close to 100 as possible.
MWI Addition Strategies: Changing the Numbers

UNIT 3 | **141** | SESSION 2.2   © Pearson Education 3

NAME

DATE

Pairs That Make 100

1 Connect the pairs of numbers that make 100.

47	36
31	42
64	69
72	7
12	28
93	53
58	88

2 Complete these equations.

_____ + 45 = 100

32 + _____ = 100

17 + _____ = 100

_____ + 78 = 100

3 Write pairs of numbers that make 100.

_____ + _____ = 100

_____ + _____ = 100

_____ + _____ = 100

_____ + _____ = 100

NOTE

Students practice finding combinations of 2-digit numbers that add to 100.

MWI Addition Strategies: Adding by Place

NAME

DATE

Rounding to Tens

Use the number lines to help you answer the problems.

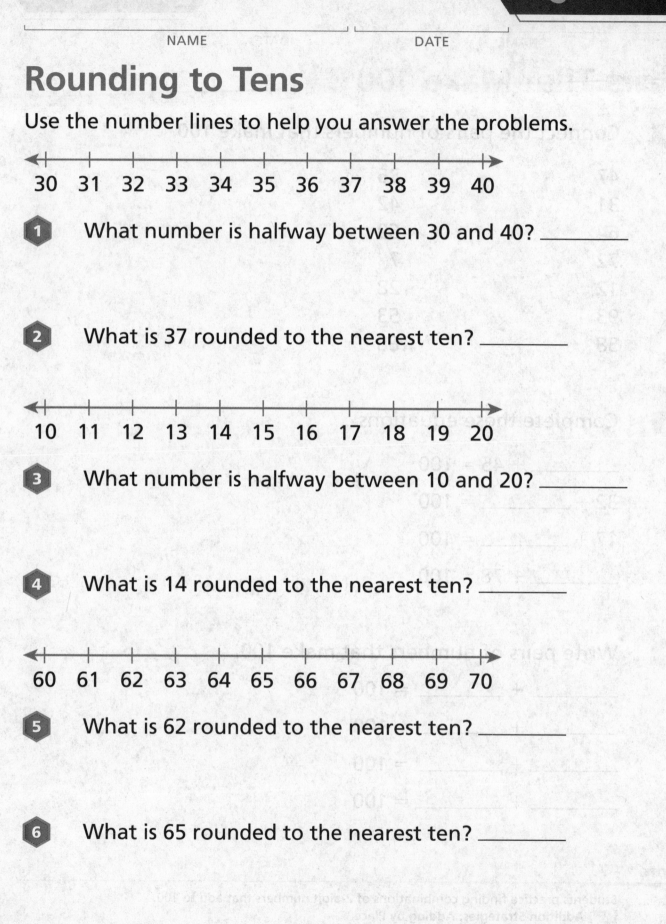

30 31 32 33 34 35 36 37 38 39 40

1 What number is halfway between 30 and 40? _____

2 What is 37 rounded to the nearest ten? _____

10 11 12 13 14 15 16 17 18 19 20

3 What number is halfway between 10 and 20? _____

4 What is 14 rounded to the nearest ten? _____

60 61 62 63 64 65 66 67 68 69 70

5 What is 62 rounded to the nearest ten? _____

6 What is 65 rounded to the nearest ten? _____

NAME _____ DATE _____

Rounding to Hundreds

Use the number lines to help you answer the problems.

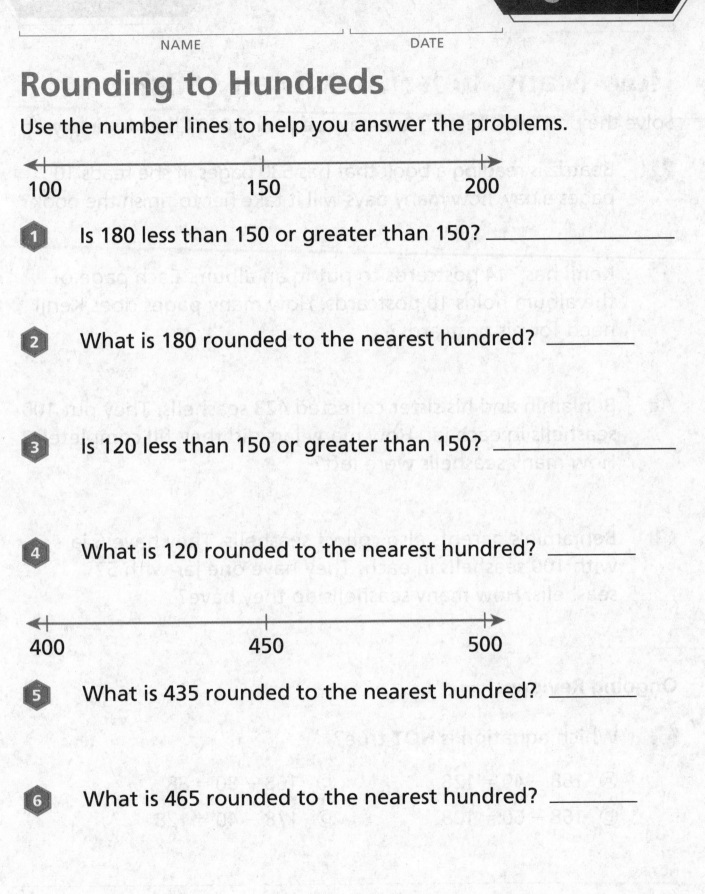

```
◄─┼────────────┼────────────┼─►
 100          150          200
```

1 Is 180 less than 150 or greater than 150? _____

2 What is 180 rounded to the nearest hundred? _____

3 Is 120 less than 150 or greater than 150? _____

4 What is 120 rounded to the nearest hundred? _____

```
◄─┼────────────┼────────────┼─►
 400          450          500
```

5 What is 435 rounded to the nearest hundred? _____

6 What is 465 rounded to the nearest hundred? _____

NAME

DATE

How Many 100s? How Many 10s?

Solve the problems below. You may use your 1,000 Chart to help you.

1 Beatriz is reading a book that has 530 pages. If she reads 10 pages a day, how many days will it take her to finish the book?

2 Kenji has 714 postcards to put in an album. Each page of the album holds 10 postcards. How many pages does Kenji need for his postcards?

3 Benjamin and his sister collected 423 seashells. They put 100 seashells in each jar. How many jars did they fill completely? How many seashells were left?

4 Benjamin's parents also collect seashells. They have 6 jars with 100 seashells in each. They have one jar with 57 seashells. How many seashells do they have?

Ongoing Review

5 Which equation is **NOT** true?

Ⓐ 168 − 40 = 128   Ⓒ 168 − 80 = 88

Ⓑ 168 − 60 = 108   Ⓓ 178 − 40 = 128

NOTE

Students find the number of 10s and 100s in 3-digit numbers.
MWI Ones, Tens, and Hundreds

NAME _____   DATE _____

How Many 10s? Part 2

1 Ms. Ahmed went to Sticker Station and bought strips of 10 stickers to give to her students. She bought 250 stickers. How many strips of 10 did she buy?

2 Gina and her brother are collecting pennies at home. They have 382 pennies so far. If they trade the pennies for dimes, how many dimes will they have? How many pennies will be left over?

3 At the end of Week 3, Ms. Santos's class had 629 bottle caps in their class collection. They are displaying the bottle caps in bags of 10. How many bags of 10 do they have? How many bottle caps are left over?

NOTE

Students find how many groups of 10 are in some 3-digit numbers.
MWI Ones, Tens, and Hundreds

Collecting Stickers and Pennies

For each problem, write an equation, solve the problem, and show your solution. Remember that stickers come in sheets of 100, strips of 10, and as single stickers.

1 Oscar collects animal stickers. He has 135 stickers in his collection. With his birthday money, he buys 1 sheet, 1 strip, and 2 single stickers to add to his collection. How many animal stickers does Oscar have now?

2 Gina collects dog stickers. In her sticker book, she has 2 full pages of 100 stickers and 1 page with 7 single stickers. For her birthday, her friends give her 4 strips and 8 single dog stickers. How many dog stickers does Gina have now?

3 Jung collects sports stickers. In her sticker box, she has 258 soccer stickers. She also has 127 tennis stickers. How many soccer and tennis stickers does Jung have in all?

Collecting Stickers and Pennies

For each problem, write an equation, solve the problem, and show your solution.

Remember to write your answers as dollars and cents.

 4 Last month, Lucas collected 97 pennies. This month, he collected 143 pennies. How much money does Lucas have now?

 5 Kim had $2.64 in her penny collection. Her aunt gave her 108 more pennies. How much money does Kim have now?

6 Cristobal had 352 pennies in his collection. His younger brother had 49¢ in his penny collection. How much money did they have in all?

NAME

DATE

94 Stickers

Solve the problems below and show your work.
Write an equation for each combination of strips
and singles. The first equation is started for you.

1   Arthur bought 94 stickers at Sticker Station.
He bought 9 strips of 10 and some singles.
How many singles did he buy?

$90 + \underline{\hspace{2cm}} = 94$

2   Keith bought 94 stickers as well. He bought
8 strips of 10 and some singles. How many
singles did he buy?

3   David also bought 94 stickers. He bought
2 strips of 10 and many singles. How many
singles did he buy?

4   Deondra bought 94 stickers, too. She bought
some strips of 10 and 34 singles. How many
strips of 10 did she buy?

NOTE

Students practice making the number 94 with different combinations of 10s and 1s.
MWI **Many Ways to Make 145**

Combining Collections

1 If these two baseball cap collections were put together, how many baseball caps would there be in all? First, make an estimate. Then, write an equation, solve the problem, and show your solution below.

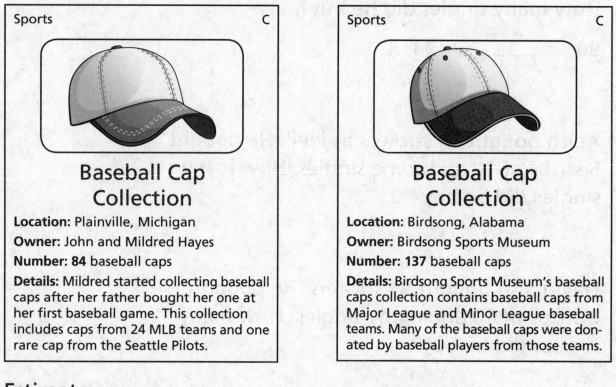

Sports	C
Baseball Cap Collection	

Location: Plainville, Michigan
Owner: John and Mildred Hayes
Number: 84 baseball caps
Details: Mildred started collecting baseball caps after her father bought her one at her first baseball game. This collection includes caps from 24 MLB teams and one rare cap from the Seattle Pilots.

Sports	C
Baseball Cap Collection	

Location: Birdsong, Alabama
Owner: Birdsong Sports Museum
Number: 137 baseball caps
Details: Birdsong Sports Museum's baseball caps collection contains baseball caps from Major League and Minor League baseball teams. Many of the baseball caps were donated by baseball players from those teams.

Estimate: _____

Equation: _____

How did you solve the problem?

Combining Collections

2   If these two dragonfly collections were put together, how many dragonflies would there be in all? First, make an estimate. Then, write an equation, solve the problem, and show your solution below.

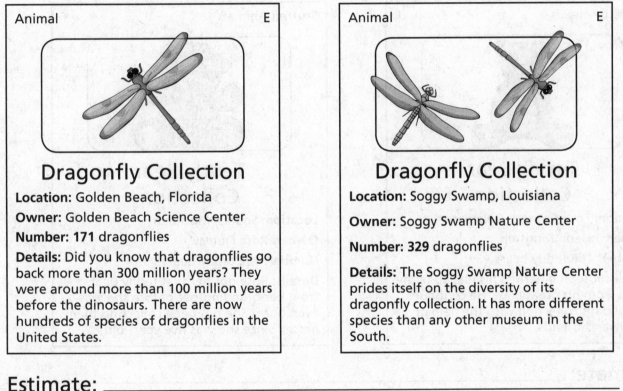

Animal   E

Dragonfly Collection

Location: Golden Beach, Florida

Owner: Golden Beach Science Center

Number: 171 dragonflies

Details: Did you know that dragonflies go back more than 300 million years? They were around more than 100 million years before the dinosaurs. There are now hundreds of species of dragonflies in the United States.

Animal   E

Dragonfly Collection

Location: Soggy Swamp, Louisiana

Owner: Soggy Swamp Nature Center

Number: 329 dragonflies

Details: The Soggy Swamp Nature Center prides itself on the diversity of its dragonfly collection. It has more different species than any other museum in the South.

Estimate: _____

Equation: _____

How did you solve the problem?

Combining Collections

3 If these two teddy-bear collections were put together, how many teddy bears would there be in all? First, make an estimate. Then write an equation, solve the problem, and show your solution below.

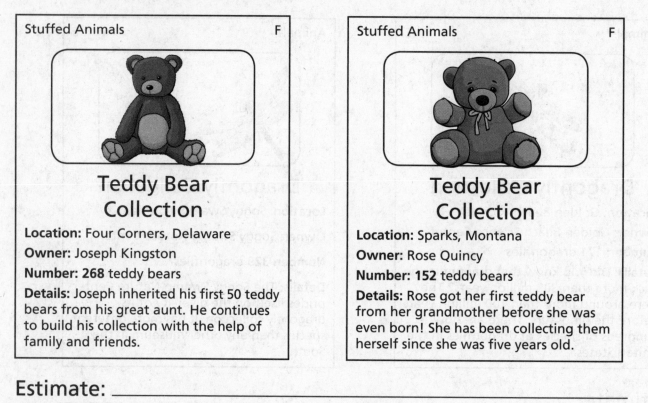

Stuffed Animals   F

Teddy Bear Collection

Location: Four Corners, Delaware

Owner: Joseph Kingston

Number: 268 teddy bears

Details: Joseph inherited his first 50 teddy bears from his great aunt. He continues to build his collection with the help of family and friends.

Stuffed Animals   F

Teddy Bear Collection

Location: Sparks, Montana

Owner: Rose Quincy

Number: 152 teddy bears

Details: Rose got her first teddy bear from her grandmother before she was even born! She has been collecting them herself since she was five years old.

Estimate: _____

Equation: _____

How did you solve the problem?

NAME _____ DATE _____

Addition Problems

Solve each problem and show your solution. Write an equation to go with the story problem.

 1 The cafeteria received 285 cartons of milk today. 134 cartons of milk were left from yesterday. How many cartons of milk does the cafeteria have to sell today?

 2 $391 + 88 = $ _____

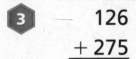 **3**
$$\begin{array}{r} 126 \\ +\ 275 \\ \hline \end{array}$$

Ongoing Review

4 Which expression does **NOT** equal 100?

Ⓐ $65 + 35$ Ⓒ $13 + 87$

Ⓑ $48 + 52$ Ⓓ $29 + 81$

NOTE

Students solve addition problems with 2- and 3-digit numbers.
MWI Addition Strategies: Adding by Place

NAME   DATE

Combining Stamp Collections

Write an equation, solve the
problem, and show your solution.

Stamps	#9

Canadian Stamp Collection

Location: Greenville, Connecticut

Owner: Greenville City Museum

Number: 145 stamps

Details: Greenville is home to a large community of French Canadians. The Canadian Stamp Collection was created from the donations of local collectors.

Stamps	#10

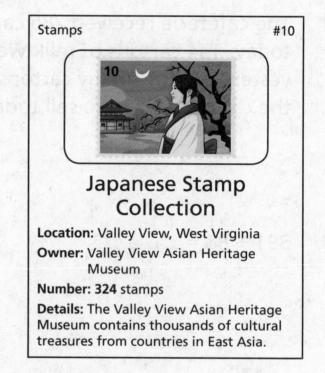

Japanese Stamp Collection

Location: Valley View, West Virginia

Owner: Valley View Asian Heritage Museum

Number: 324 stamps

Details: The Valley View Asian Heritage Museum contains thousands of cultural treasures from countries in East Asia.

The Greenville City Museum is loaning its stamp collection to the Valley View Asian Heritage Museum for a special showing. When the two collections are combined, how many stamps will there be in all?

NOTE

Students practice solving addition problems with 3-digit numbers.

MWI Addition Strategies: Adding One Number in Parts

NAME

DATE

Rounding Numbers to 10s and 100s

Round each number to the nearest ten and hundred.

 238

What is 238 rounded to the nearest ten? _____

What is 238 rounded to the nearest hundred? _____

 453

What is 453 rounded to the nearest ten? _____

What is 453 rounded to the nearest hundred? _____

 317

What is 317 rounded to the nearest ten? _____

What is 317 rounded to the nearest hundred? _____

 639

What is 639 rounded to the nearest ten? _____

What is 639 rounded to the nearest hundred? _____

 702

What is 702 rounded to the nearest ten? _____

What is 702 rounded to the nearest hundred? _____

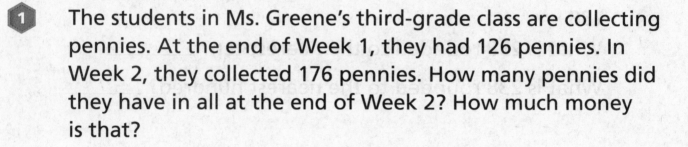
Collections Story Problems

For each problem, write an equation, solve the problem, and show your solution.

1 The students in Ms. Greene's third-grade class are collecting pennies. At the end of Week 1, they had 126 pennies. In Week 2, they collected 176 pennies. How many pennies did they have in all at the end of Week 2? How much money is that?

2 The students in Mr. River's third-grade class are collecting bottle caps. At the end of Week 1, they had 247 bottle caps. In Week 2, they collected 184 bottle caps. How many bottle caps did they have in all at the end of Week 2?

3 Jane and Ines both have stamp collections. Jane has 135 stamps in her collection, and Ines has 229 stamps in her collection. They brought their collections to school to show their class. How many stamps did the two girls have in all?

4 In Ms. Silvie's third-grade class, many of the students collect stickers. The boys in the class have 158 stickers and the girls in the class have 302 stickers. How many stickers do Ms. Silvie's third graders have in all?

NAME _____   DATE _____

More Rounding

For each problem, write the number in expanded form and round it to the nearest ten or hundred.

 1   **138**

Expanded form _____

What is 138 rounded to the nearest ten? _____

What is 138 rounded to the nearest hundred? _____

 2   **459**

Expanded form _____

What is 459 rounded to the nearest ten? _____

What is 459 rounded to the nearest hundred? _____

 3   **392**

Expanded form _____

What is 392 rounded to the nearest ten? _____

What is 392 rounded to the nearest hundred? _____

 4   **750**

Expanded form _____

What is 750 rounded to the nearest ten? _____

What is 750 rounded to the nearest hundred? _____

NOTE

Students write numbers in expanded form and round them to the nearest ten and hundred.
MWI **Round Whole 3-Digit Numbers**

© Pearson Education 3

NAME   DATE

Solving Addition Problems

Solve each problem and show your solution. For Problem 3, write an equation to go with the story problem.

 1 $215 + 78 = $ _____

 2 $157 + 121 = $ _____

3   The students in Ms. Suarez's class had 320 bottle caps in their collection at the end of last week. This week, the students collected 64 more bottle caps. How many bottle caps do they have now?

NOTE

Students practice solving addition problems with 2- and 3-digit numbers.
MWI Addition Strategies: Adding by Place

Addition Starter Problems

In each set of problems below, solve all three
Starter Problems. Then solve the final problem, and
show your solution. If you used a Starter Problem
to help you solve the final problem, tell which one.

 100 + 100 = _____

146 + 100 = _____

140 + 120 = _____

146 + 124 = _____

 200 + 100 = _____

263 + 7 = _____

260 + 130 = _____

263 + 139 = _____

Addition Starter Problems

In each set of problems below, solve all three
Starter Problems. Then solve the final problem, and
show your solution. If you used a Starter Problem
to help you solve the final problem, tell which one.

  $100 + 300 =$ _____

$316 + 100 =$ _____

$130 + 310 =$ _____

$137 + 316 =$ _____

  $100 + 200 =$ _____

$154 + 200 =$ _____

$150 + 240 =$ _____

$154 + 248 =$ _____

Addition Starter Problems

In each set of problems below, solve all three
Starter Problems. Then solve the final problem, and
show your solution. If you used a Starter Problem
to help you solve the final problem, tell which one.

 5 $200 + 100 = $ _____

$271 + 100 = $ _____

$271 + 200 = $ _____

$271 + 199 = $ _____

 6 $200 + 300 = $ _____

$220 + 350 = $ _____

$225 + 350 = $ _____

$225 + 357 = $ _____

NAME _____ DATE _____

Fisherman's Log

Fishermen log how many fish they catch each day. Use this fisherman's log to solve the problems below. Write an equation and show your solution for each problem.

Day	Monday	Tuesday	Wednesday	Thursday
Count	276	230	239	257

1

a. How many fish did the fisherman catch on Monday and Tuesday?

b. How many fish did the fisherman catch on Wednesday and Thursday?

c. The fisherman's weekly goal is to catch 1,000 fish. Did he meet his goal? How far over or under is he from his goal?

Ongoing Review

2 Which number makes the equation true?

$36 +$ _____ $= 100$

Ⓐ 55   Ⓑ 64   Ⓒ 74   Ⓓ 76

NOTE

Students practice solving addition problems with 3-digit numbers.
MWI Subtraction Strategies: Adding Up and Subtracting Back

NAME   DATE

Adding and Subtracting Multiples of 10 and 100

Solve each set of problems below.

1   125 + 100 = _____

125 + 200 = _____

125 + 300 = _____

2   346 − 100 = _____

346 − 200 = _____

346 − 300 = _____

3   207 + 40 = _____

207 + 60 = _____

207 + 80 = _____

4   172 − 50 = _____

172 − 70 = _____

172 − 90 = _____

NOTE

Students practice adding and subtracting multiples of 10 and 100.

MWI Adding and Subtracting Tens and Hundreds

More Starter Problems

In each set of problems below, solve all three Starter Problems. Then solve the final problem, and show your solution. If you used a Starter Problem to help you solve the final problem, tell which one.

1 $200 + 300 =$ _____

$317 + 300 =$ _____

$17 + 58 =$ _____

$217 + 358 =$ _____

2 $100 + 298 =$ _____

$119 + 300 =$ _____

$100 + 200 =$ _____

$119 + 298 =$ _____

Ongoing Review

3 Which equation is **NOT** true?

Ⓐ $35 + 43 = 80$ Ⓒ $63 + 17 = 80$

Ⓑ $25 + 55 = 80$ Ⓓ $45 + 35 = 80$

NOTE

Students solve Starter Problems and then use one of the Starter Problems to solve the final problem.

MWI **Addition Strategies: Changing the Numbers**

Distance Riddles

Solve the riddles below. Put the two numbers you find on the number line. Then find the difference between each pair of numbers. Write the addition and subtraction equations that show the distance between the numbers.

 The distance between 100 and me is 28.

←———————————————|———————————————→
                      100

What numbers can I be?

The difference between the two numbers is _____.

Equations: _____

 The distance between 100 and me is 44.

←———————————————|———————————————→
                      100

What numbers can I be?

The difference between the two numbers is _____.

Equations: _____

Distance Riddles

3 The distance between 100 and me is 57.

100

What numbers can I be?

The difference between the two numbers is _____.

Equations: _____

4 The distance between 100 and me is 72.

100

What numbers can I be?

The difference between the two numbers is _____.

Equations: _____

5 The distance between 100 and me is 63.

100

What numbers can I be?

The difference between the two numbers is _____.

Equations: _____

NAME _____ DATE _____

Practice with Distance Riddles

Solve the riddles below. Write the two numbers you find on the number line. Then find the difference between each pair of numbers. Write the addition and subtraction equations that show the distance between the numbers.

1 The distance between 100 and me is 31.

100

What numbers can I be?

The difference between the two numbers is _____.

Equations: _____

2 The distance between 100 and me is 86.

100

What numbers can I be?

The difference between the two numbers is _____.

Equations: _____

Ongoing Review

3 There were 100 paper clips in a box. Gina used 29 clips for a project.
How many were left?

Ⓐ 81   Ⓑ 70   Ⓒ 71   Ⓓ 129

NOTE

Students find two numbers that are a given distance from 100 on the number line.
Then they find the difference between the two numbers.
MWI Solving a Multi-Step Problem

NAME   DATE

Addition Story Problems

For each problem, write an equation, solve the problem, and show your solution.

1 The South City Soccer League has 133 players on all of the teams. The Rivertown Soccer League has 148 players. When all of the players in both leagues get together for a tournament, how many players will there be?

2 The South City Soccer League bought 140 small T-shirts and 85 large T-shirts to give to the players, the parents, and the coaches. How many T-shirts did the league buy?

3 To pay for new equipment, the Rivertown Soccer League raised $161 from a bake sale and $244 from a car wash. How much money did the league raise in total?

NOTE

Students practice solving addition story problems with 2- and 3-digit numbers.
MWI Addition Strategies: Adding by Place

Travel Problems: The Santos Family Vacation

Write an equation to represent each problem.
Solve each problem and show your solution.

 Question for Keisha

When the Santos family stopped at the diner, they had traveled 36 miles from their home. At the gas station, the trip meter read 79 miles. How far did they travel from the diner to the gas station?

 Question for Edwin

The Santos family had driven 79 miles when they stopped at the gas station. How much farther will they have to drive to reach 100 miles?

Travel Problems: The Santos Family Vacation

3 Question for the Class

When the Santos family stopped at the gas station, the trip meter read 79 miles. When they arrived at their grandparents' house, it read 128 miles. How far did they travel from the gas station to their grandparents' house?

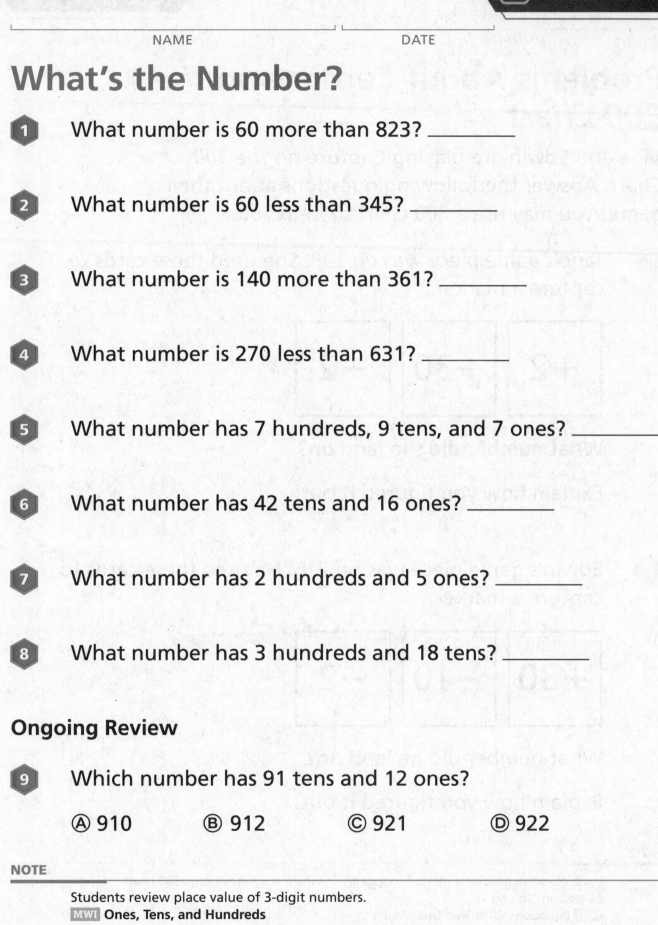

What's the Number?

1 What number is 60 more than 823? _____

2 What number is 60 less than 345? _____

3 What number is 140 more than 361? _____

4 What number is 270 less than 631? _____

5 What number has 7 hundreds, 9 tens, and 7 ones? _____

6 What number has 42 tens and 16 ones? _____

7 What number has 2 hundreds and 5 ones? _____

8 What number has 3 hundreds and 18 tens? _____

Ongoing Review

9 Which number has 91 tens and 12 ones?

Ⓐ 910   Ⓑ 912   Ⓒ 921   Ⓓ 922

NOTE

Students review place value of 3-digit numbers.
MWI **Ones, Tens, and Hundreds**

NAME _____ DATE _____

Problems About *Capture on the 300 Chart*

Jane and Edwin are playing *Capture on the 300 Chart*. Answer the following questions about their game. You may use a 300 chart to help you.

 1 Jane's game piece was on 139. She used these cards to capture a marker:

+2   +30   +2

What number did she land on?

Explain how you figured it out.

 2 Edwin's game piece was on 216. He used these cards to capture a marker:

+30   −10   −2

What number did he land on?

Explain how you figured it out.

NOTE

Students solve problems related to a game in which they move on a 300 chart by adding 10s and 1s.
MWI Equations With Two Operations

NAME _____ DATE _____

More Distance Riddles

1 I am 20 less than 100. What number am I?
I am 52 more than 100. What number am I?

100

What is the difference between these two numbers? Write an addition equation *and* a subtraction equation that show this difference.

2 I am 35 less than 100. What number am I?
I am 25 more than 100. What number am I?

100

What is the difference between these two numbers? Write an addition equation *and* a subtraction equation that show this difference.

3 I am 42 less than 100. What number am I?
I am 18 more than 100. What number am I?

100

What is the difference between these two numbers? Write an addition equation *and* a subtraction equation that show this difference.

More Travel Problems

Write an equation to represent each problem.
Then solve each one and show your solutions.

1 Last weekend, the McDonald family took
the train to Center City. The train traveled
16 miles before stopping at the White Pines
station to pick up more passengers. When
the train pulled into the Center City station,
it had traveled 93 miles in all. How far did
the train travel from the White Pines station
to Center City?

2 The Chan family visited their cousins last
summer. They set the trip meter on their car
at 0 before they left home. They stopped at
a rest area 42 miles from their home. Later,
they stopped to get lunch at a restaurant
100 miles from their home. How far did they
travel from the rest area to the restaurant?

More Travel Problems

3 When the Chan family arrived at their cousins' house, the trip meter read 138 miles. How far did they travel from the rest area to their cousins' house?

NAME _____   DATE _____

Biking Trip

Write an equation, solve each problem, and show your solution for each problem.

 1

a. Philip and Keith are on a 3-day biking trip. Their final destination is 138 miles away. On the first day, they rode 51 miles. How much farther do they have to bike?

b. On the second day, they biked through some steep hills and rode only 37 miles. How far have they biked so far?

c. How much farther do they have to bike to reach their destination?

Ongoing Review

2 Which number makes the equation true?

$69 + \underline{\hspace{2cm}} = 143$

Ⓐ 64   Ⓑ 74   Ⓒ 84   Ⓓ 86

NOTE

Students solve distance problems to practice subtraction.
MWI Subtraction Strategies: Adding Up and Subtracting Back

NAME

DATE

Addition Practice

For each problem, write an equation, solve the problem, and show your solution.

1 Last summer, the Smith family traveled to their cousins' house. The trip took two days. They drove 246 miles on the first day of their trip and 318 miles on the second day. How far did they travel in all?

2 The West Side Toy Museum has 372 toy cars in its collection. Mr. Jones is donating his collection of 153 toy cars to the museum. How many cars will the West Side Toy Museum have then?

3 The students in a third-grade class at Beech Street School collected 298 pennies the first week of their class collection. They collected 282 pennies the second week. How many pennies in total did the students collect in the first two weeks of their class collection?

NOTE

Students practice solving story problems involving the addition of 3-digit numbers. Ask your child to explain how he or she solved each problem.
MWI Addition Strategies: Adding One Number in Parts

NAME
DATE

Sticker Station

For each problem, write an equation that represents what the problem is asking. Then solve the problem and show your work.

1   **a.** Gina went to Sticker Station and bought 164 lion stickers and 30 boat stickers. How many stickers did she buy?

       b. Gina went back the next day and bought 33 more stickers. How many does she have now?

2   David had 186 stickers. He gave 41 stickers to his best friend, Nancy. How many stickers does David have now?

3   Philip had 179 stickers. He went to Sticker Station and bought 65 more stickers. How many stickers does Philip have now?

NOTE

Students practice adding and subtracting 2-digit numbers.
MWI Subtraction Strategies: Adding Up and Subtracting Back

More Trips Home

Solve the problems below. Be sure to show how you got your answer. Write equations that show what you did.

 1   Last summer, the Soeng family visited an amusement park 136 miles from their home. Returning home by the same route, they stopped to see their aunt. She lives 72 miles from their home. How far is it from the amusement park to their aunt's home?

2   During spring vacation, the Davis family drove 152 miles to visit the science museum in their state capital. Returning home by the same route, they stopped at the Dinosaur Tracks State Park. The park is 43 miles from their home. How far was the drive from the science museum to the State Park?

More Trips Home

3 Last weekend, the Smith family drove 179 miles to Ocean Beach State Park. On the same route home, they stopped for dinner at the Green Mountain Family Restaurant. The restaurant is 65 miles from their home. How far was the drive from Ocean Beach State Park to the restaurant?

Marbles

For each problem, write an equation that represents what the problem is asking. Then solve the problem and show your work.

1 Richard has 253 green marbles and 128 orange marbles. How many marbles does he have altogether?

2 Christopher had 268 marbles. His uncle gave him 120 marbles and his cousin gave him 30 marbles. How many marbles does Christopher have now?

3 Kim had 189 marbles. She gave 42 marbles to her sister. How many marbles does Kim have now?

Ongoing Review

4 Which clock shows 6:36?

Ⓐ   Ⓑ   Ⓒ   Ⓓ

NOTE

Students write equations and solve addition and subtraction story problems.
MWI Solving a Multi-Step Problem

Comparing Lengths and Heights

For each problem, write an equation, solve the problem, and show your solution. You may use cubes, number lines, or drawings to help you solve the problem or explain your thinking.

1

a. Ms. Martinez is 67 inches tall. Philip is 52 inches tall. How much taller is Ms. Martinez than Philip?

b. A basketball player is 82 inches tall. How much taller is the basketball player than Ms. Martinez?

c. How much would Philip have to grow to be as tall as the basketball player?

Comparing Lengths and Heights

There are many reptiles at the Frederick Zoo. The data table shows some of the reptiles and their lengths in centimeters. Use the information in the table to write and solve an equation for each problem. Show your solutions on a separate piece of paper.

Kind of Reptile	Length in Centimeters
American alligator	260 centimeters
Veiled chameleon	53 centimeters
Eastern ratsnake	128 centimeters

2 How much longer is the eastern ratsnake than the veiled chameleon?

_____

3 **a.** Which reptile in this table is the longest?

_____

Which reptile in this table is the shortest?

_____

b. How much would the shortest reptile have to grow to be as long as the longest reptile?

_____

© Pearson Education 3

NAME

DATE

Feeding Animals

Solve the following story problems. Show
your work.

 1 At one stable, horses are fed carrot sticks
each morning. Each horse eats 6 carrot sticks.
How many carrot sticks will 4 horses eat?

2 Horses also like to eat apple slices as treats.
The stable keeper has 48 apple slices for
6 horses. How many apple slices will each
horse get if they are shared equally?

3 Fuzzy is the pet rabbit in Ms. Thom's
classroom. Fuzzy eats 3 lettuce leaves
each day.

a. How many leaves will Fuzzy eat in 6 days?

b. How many leaves will Fuzzy eat in 9 days?

NOTE

Students solve multiplication and division story problems.
MWI Solving Multiplication Problems

NAME   DATE

Comparing Collections: How Many More?

For each problem, write an equation, solve the problem, and show your solution.

 1   Denzel and Jung each collect marbles. Denzel has 104 marbles, and Jung has 65 marbles. How many more marbles does Denzel have than Jung?

2   Keith has 92 stickers in his sticker book. Nancy has 58 stickers in her book. How many more stickers does Keith have than Nancy?

3   Ms. Santos's class collected 86 bottle caps. Mr. Singh's class collected 123 bottle caps. How many more bottle caps did Mr. Singh's class collect than Ms. Santos's class?

 4   The Ocean Park Aquarium has 95 tropical fish and 67 jellyfish in its collection. How many more tropical fish than jellyfish does the aquarium have?

© Pearson Education 3

NAME

DATE

Oldest Animals

The animals in the table lived a record number of years.

Animal	Record Ages
Parrot	35 years
Monkey	53 years
Alligator	66 years
Eel	88 years

1 How many more years did the oldest monkey live than the oldest parrot?

2 How many more years did the oldest eel live than the oldest alligator?

3 A young alligator is 9 years old.

a. How many more years will it need to live to tie the record for the oldest alligator?

b. Explain the strategy you used to find the answer.

Ongoing Review

4 How much longer did the oldest eel live than the oldest parrot?

Ⓐ 35 years   Ⓑ 50 years   Ⓒ 53 years   Ⓓ 55 years

NOTE

Students solve comparison problems to practice subtraction.
MWI Subtraction Situations

NAME _____ DATE _____

All About the Number

Answer the following questions about the number 432.
You may use your 1,000 Chart to help you.

 1 Is 432 closer to 400 or 500? _____
How do you know?

 2 Choose a landmark number that is close to 432.

_____

 3 Is 432 more or less than that landmark number?

_____

 4 How many 100s are in 432? _____

 5 How many 10s are in 432?

_____

 6 What number is 30 more than 432? _____

 7 What number is 20 less than 432? _____

NOTE
_____

Students use a 1,000 Chart to answer questions about a given 3-digit number.
MWI **Tools to Represent Subtraction Problems**

Related Problems

Solve the problems. Think about how solving the first one in each set might help you solve the others. Show your solutions. Write equations for the story problems.

Set 1. Kelley had 88 pennies in her piggy bank. She spent 50¢ on a get-well card for her grandmother. How much money does Kelley have left?

Nicholas's mom gave him the loose change from her purse, which came to 88¢. He spent 40¢ on a sticker for his collection. How much money does Nicholas have left?

Set 2.	$95 - 30 = \underline{\hspace{2cm}}$	**Set 3.**	100	105	115
	$95 - 20 = \underline{\hspace{2cm}}$		$-\ 70$	$-\ 70$	$-\ 70$
	$95 - 15 = \underline{\hspace{2cm}}$				
Set 4.	$160 - 20 = \underline{\hspace{2cm}}$	**Set 5.**	135	135	135
	$160 - 25 = \underline{\hspace{2cm}}$		$-\ 30$	$-\ 40$	$-\ 38$
	$160 - 27 = \underline{\hspace{2cm}}$				

© Pearson Education 3

Related Problems

Solve the problems. Think about how solving the first one in each set might help you solve the others. Show your solutions. Write equations for the story problems.

Set 6. Bridget has 100 stickers. Gil has 67 stickers. How many more stickers does Gil need to have the same number as Bridget?

On Monday, Mr. Li's students brought in 112 pennies for their Class Collection. Ms. Trenton's students brought in 67 pennies on the same day. How many more pennies did the students in Mr. Li's class bring to school than the students in Ms. Trenton's class?

Set 7. $100 - 50 =$ _____	**Set 8.** $\begin{array}{r} 200 \\ -150 \end{array}$ $\begin{array}{r} 210 \\ -150 \end{array}$ $\begin{array}{r} 210 \\ -145 \end{array}$
$120 - 50 =$ _____	
$120 - 54 =$ _____	
Set 9. $230 - 100 =$ _____	**Set 10.** $\begin{array}{r} 300 \\ -25 \end{array}$ $\begin{array}{r} 301 \\ -25 \end{array}$ $\begin{array}{r} 310 \\ -25 \end{array}$
$230 - 90 =$ _____	
$230 - 95 =$ _____	

Choose one set of problems from among the Related Problems, Sets 1–10. On a separate sheet of paper, explain how you used each problem in the set to help you solve the next problem.

How Much Longer? How Much Taller?

For each problem, write an equation, solve the problem, and show your solution.

1 The Burmese python at the Riverview Zoo is 132 inches long. The boa constrictor is 87 inches long. How much longer is the Burmese python than the boa constrictor?

2 Keisha is 54 inches tall. Her younger sister Mimi is 37 inches tall. How much would Mimi need to grow to be as tall as Keisha is now?

3 Anna and Gil are growing sunflowers in their gardens. Anna's sunflower is 116 inches tall. Gil's sunflower is 49 inches tall. How much taller is Anna's sunflower than Gil's sunflower?

NAME

DATE

Picking Apples

Solve each problem. Show your work and write an equation.

1 While she was at the farm, Amy picked 62 apples in the morning and 54 apples in the afternoon. How many apples did Amy pick in all?

2 Adam picked 73 apples in the morning and 47 apples in the afternoon. How many apples did Adam pick in all?

3 Lana picked 86 apples at the farm. When she got home, she added these to the 55 apples she had picked the day before. How many apples does she have in all?

NOTE

Students practice adding 2-digit numbers.
MWI Addition Strategies: Adding One Number in Parts

How Many Are Left?

For each problem, write an equation, solve the problem, and show your solution.

Remember that there are 100 stickers on a sheet and 10 stickers on a strip.

1 Kathryn had 5 sheets of baseball stickers. She gave 40 stickers to her friend for a birthday present. How many stickers did Kathryn have left?

2 Edwin had 3 sheets of insect stickers. He gave 12 dragonfly stickers to the science teacher. How many stickers did Edwin have left?

3 Gil had 2 sheets and 5 strips of famous-people stickers. He sold 65 of them at a yard sale. How many stickers did Gil have left?

4 Kelley had 4 sheets of cat stickers. Her dog chewed up 2 sheets, plus 47 more from another sheet. How many stickers did Kelley have left?

How Many Are Left?

For each problem, write an equation, solve the problem, and show your solution.

 5 The Greenville City Museum had 145 stamps in its Canadian stamp collection. The museum sold 60 of them to another collector. How many are left?

 6 Ms. Heston had 253 puzzles in her collection. She sold 130 of them to the children's museum. How many are left?

 7 The Flagtown Aquarium had 282 tropical fish in its collection. Last winter 106 got sick and died. How many are left?

 8 Mr. Aboud had 222 basketball trading cards in his collection. He gave 182 of them to his niece and nephew. How many are left?

NAME

DATE

Parking Garage

The parking attendant keeps a log of the number of cars parked in the garage each day. The table shows the count for last week.

Use the information about the parking garage. For Problems 2 and 3, write an equation, solve the problem, and show your solution.

Day	Number of Cars
Sunday	178
Monday	224
Tuesday	230
Wednesday	237
Thursday	215
Friday	261
Saturday	268

1. Write the number of cars in order, from the least to the greatest, on the number line below.

2. How many more cars were parked on Saturday than on Sunday?

_____

3. The maximum capacity of the garage is 305 cars. How many more cars could have been parked on Monday?

_____

NOTE

Students order and subtract with 3-digit numbers.
MWI **Ones, Tens, and Hundreds**

NAME

DATE

How Far From 100? Story Problems

Solve the problems below. Be sure to show how you got your answers. Write equations that show what you did.

 1 Oscar and Becky are playing *How Far From 100?* In Round 1, Becky is dealt the following cards:

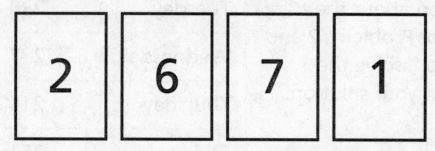

Becky says that 126 is the closest 3-digit number to 100 that she can make. Is there a 2-digit number she can make that will get her closer to 100?

2 While playing *How Far From 100?*, Mia makes a number that is 31 away from 100. What could her number be? Gil makes a different number that is 31 away from 100. What could his number be?

3 Elena makes a number that is 19 away from 100. What two numbers could she have made? Explain how you know.

NOTE

Students find 2- and 3-digit numbers that are close to 100.
MWI Ones, Tens, and Hundreds

© Pearson Education 3

Solving Subtraction Problems

Solve the following problems and show your solutions. Write an equation for the story problem.

1   242 − 160 = _____

2   Ms. Santos's class has collected 208 cans for the third grade's recycling project. Mr. Rivers's class has collected 88 cans. How many more cans has Ms. Santos's class collected?

3   168
     − 73
     ‾‾‾‾

4   Write a story for this problem, and then solve the problem.

     194 − 112 = _____

NAME   DATE

Subtraction Problems

Solve each problem and show your solution.

1 184 − 65 = _____

2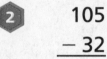
   105
  − 32

3 274 − 159 = _____

Ongoing Review

4 Which expression does **NOT** equal 100?

   Ⓐ 135 − 40 + 5

   Ⓑ 68 + 50 − 20 + 2

   Ⓒ 75 + 40 − 25

   Ⓓ 66 + 50 − 10 − 10 + 4

NOTE

Students solve subtraction problems.
MWI Subtraction Strategies: Subtracting One Number in Parts

© Pearson Education 3

NAME _____ DATE _____

Addition and Subtraction Practice

Solve the following problems and show your solutions.

1   145 + 68 = _____

2   227 + 114 = _____

3   171 − 83 = _____

4   250 − 166 = _____

NOTE

Students practice solving addition and subtraction problems with 2- and 3-digit numbers.
MWI Subtraction Strategies: Adding Up and Subtracting Back

UNIT 3 | **203** | SESSION 5.5   © Pearson Education 3

NAME

DATE

Addition and Subtraction Word Problems

Write an equation for each word problem.
Solve the equations and show your solutions.

1 Margery collects stickers. She received 125 cat stickers and some money on her birthday. Later that day, she used some of the money to buy 1 sheet, 7 strips, and 6 single flower stickers at Sticker Station. How many stickers did she add to her collection on her birthday?

2 Over the weekend, Aaron read 107 pages of a book. His twin sister Ashley read 234 pages of the same book. How many more pages did Ashley read than Aaron?

3 Jordy has 119 pennies in his piggy bank. Calvin had 291 pennies in his piggy bank, but he exchanged 200 pennies for 2 dollar bills. How many total pennies do Jordy and Calvin have now?

NOTE

Students solve addition and subtraction word problems.
MWI Solving a Multi-Step Problem

Perimeter, Area, and Polygons

Perimeter, Area, and Polygons

Finding Lengths

Use a ruler, yardstick, and meter stick to find objects that are about the same length as these measurement units. Record the objects that you find for each unit.

Centimeter	Inch
Example: The tip of my pencil	
Foot	**Yard/Meter**

NAME

DATE

What's the Number?

Answer the following questions.

1   What number is 50 more than 824? _____

2   What number is 40 less than 567? _____

3   What number is 80 more than 365? _____

4   What number is 30 less than 215? _____

5   What number is 200 more than 439? _____

6   What number has 5 hundreds, 3 tens, and 2 ones? _____

7   What number has 31 tens and no ones? _____

8   What number has 6 hundreds and 8 ones? _____

9   What number has 4 hundreds and 13 tens? _____

10   What number has 16 tens and 15 ones? _____

NOTE

Students work on place value in relation to addition or subtraction of 3-digit numbers.
MWI One, Tens, and Hundreds

HOMEWORK

Choosing Measurement Tools and Units

What measurement tool (ruler, yardstick, or meter stick) would you use for each situation? What unit of measure (centimeter, inch, foot, yard, or meter) would you use?

Explain why you chose that tool and that unit of measure.

1 I need to know the length of a fence that will go around the basketball court.

Tool: _____ Unit of Measure: _____

I chose these because . . .

2 I need to know how long the strap is on my book bag.

Tool: _____ Unit of Measure: _____

I chose these because . . .

NOTE

Students decide which measuring tool and unit of measure are most appropriate for each situation. Students will continue to measure lengths in class for the next few days.

MWI **Length Measurement Tools**

© Pearson Education 3

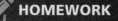
Choosing Measurement Tools and Units

3 I need to know the width of my foot at its widest point.

Tool: _____ Unit of Measure: _____

I chose these because . . .

4 I want to buy material for a bedspread. I need to know how long and how wide my bed is.

Tool: _____ Unit of Measure: _____

I chose these because . . .

NOTE

Students decide which measuring tool and unit of measure are most appropriate for each situation.

MWI **Measurement Benchmarks**

About the Mathematics in This Unit

Dear Family,

Our class is starting a new mathematics unit about geometry and measurement called *Perimeter, Area, and Polygons*. During this unit, students measure length by using U.S. standard units (inches, feet, yards) and metric units (centimeters, meters). They investigate characteristics of triangles and quadrilaterals (4-sided polygons). They use right angles as a reference to identify other angles as being greater than or less than 90 degrees. Students solve problems about perimeter (the length of the border of a figure) and area (the measure of how much flat space a figure covers).

Benchmarks	Examples
Measure and find the perimeter of 2-D figures using U.S. standard and metric units.	What is the perimeter of this photograph? 6 inches 4 inches I measured the sides of the photograph by using inches. The bottom will measure the same as the top and the right side will measure the same as the left side. $6 + 4 + 6 + 4 = 20$ The perimeter of the photograph is 20 inches.
Find the area of 2-D figures using U.S. standard and metric units.	What is the area of this figure? 8 1 2 3 4 5 6 7 I counted 7 square units and two $\frac{1}{2}$ square units, so the total area is 8 square units

About the Mathematics in This Unit

Benchmarks	Examples
Categorize quadrilaterals, including squares, rhombuses and rectangles, based on their attributes.	Which of these are quadrilaterals? Explain how you decided. 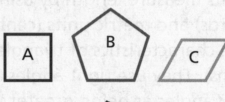  A, C, and E are quadrilaterals. They all have 4 straight sides. Which are rhombuses? A and C are rhombuses.

In our math class, students spend time discussing problems in depth and are asked to share their reasoning and solutions. It is important that children solve math problems in a way that makes sense to them. At home, encourage your child to explain the math thinking that supports those solutions.

Please look for more information and activities from Unit 4 that will be sent home in the coming weeks.

Finding and Measuring Perimeters

Choose 5 objects in the classroom that have perimeters you can measure, such as a bulletin board, the top of a table, or the side of the teacher's desk. Measure the perimeters and record your work below.

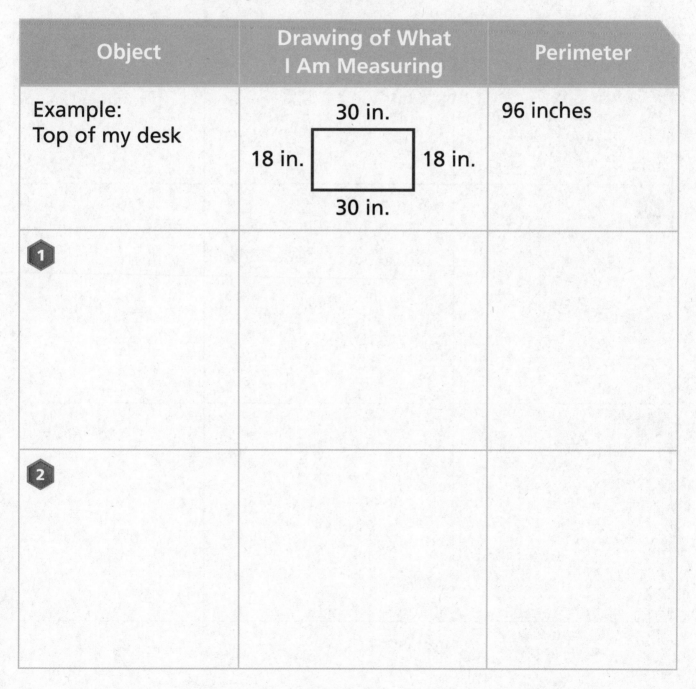

Object	Drawing of What I Am Measuring	Perimeter
Example: Top of my desk	30 in. 18 in. 18 in. 30 in.	96 inches
1		
2		

Finding and Measuring Perimeters

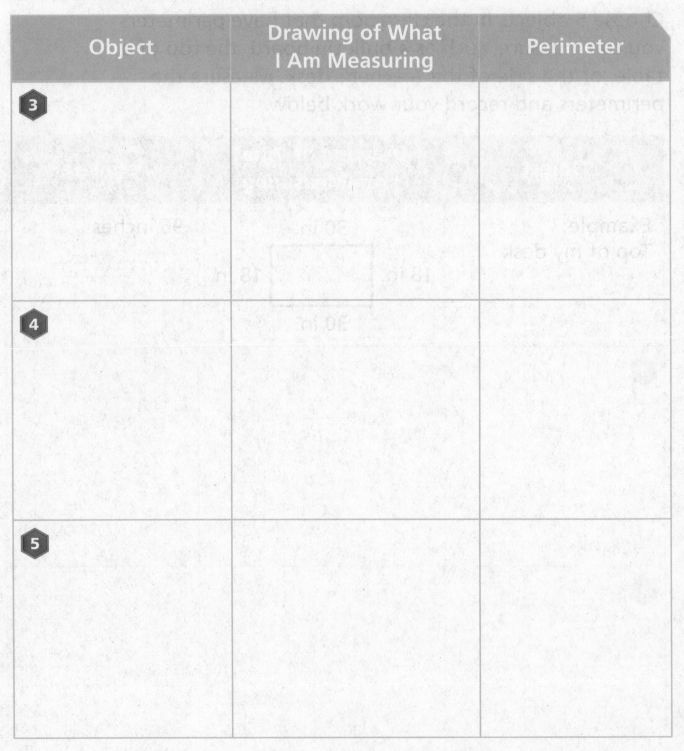

Object	Drawing of What I Am Measuring	Perimeter
3		
4		
5		

NAME _____ DATE _____

Adding 10s and 100s

Solve the following sets of related problems. Think about how you can use one problem to solve the next one.

1 368 + 30 = _____

368 + 40 = _____

368 + 50 = _____

2 449 + 100 = _____

449 + 200 = _____

449 + 300 = _____

3 267 + 40 = _____

267 + 140 = _____

267 + 240 = _____

4 582 + 10 = _____

582 + 20 = _____

582 + 30 = _____

5 506 + 30 = _____

536 + 30 = _____

566 + 30 = _____

6 434 + 150 = _____

434 + 160 = _____

434 + 170 = _____

NOTE

Students practice solving addition problems in related sets.

MWI **Adding and Subtracting Tens and Hundreds**

NAME

DATE

Perimeters at Home

Measure the perimeters of at least two objects at home.
Record your work below.

Object	Drawing of What I Am Measuring	Perimeter

NOTE

Students practice measuring the perimeter of objects, such as the top edge of the kitchen table or the front of the refrigerator door.

MWI **Perimeter**

Related Activities to Try at Home

Dear Family,

The activities below are related to the mathematics in the geometry and measurement unit *Perimeter, Area, and Polygons*. You can use the activities to enrich your child's mathematical learning experience.

Measuring Length Around the House Measurement questions occur often in our home lives. Typical questions that may come up include these: How far is it across our kitchen table? How many children can fit comfortably on the couch? What is the perimeter of the new rug, and will it fit in the bedroom? Encourage your child to estimate and measure distances in these practical situations. You may involve your child in your own measurement activities. Hobbies such as sewing and carpentry are a natural for this. You and your child can go outside to measure longer distances. How many yards is it to the end of the block? What is the distance in feet between two trees? Is the perimeter of the sandbox larger or smaller than the perimeter of the flower garden?

Measuring Area Around the House Look for opportunities at home to talk with your child about area—the two-dimensional measure of the size of a surface.

○ If you have square tiles covering a floor or bathroom wall, ask, "How many squares are there?"

○ Ask your child to help you figure out the area of a tabletop or the floor of a room by using different common objects as the unit of measure. For example, how many sheets of notebook paper would it take to cover the kitchen floor? How many index cards would it take to cover a table? Your child can estimate the answer first and then use the sheets of paper or index cards to find the exact amount.

Related Activities to Try at Home

Triangle and Quadrilateral Scavenger Hunt Look for examples
of triangles and quadrilaterals (closed shapes with 4 straight
sides) during your daily travels with your child. For example,
when you are in the car together, your child can call out
the triangles or quadrilaterals that he or she sees on signs,
buildings, shop windows, and so on.

Perimeter Problems

1 Your teacher wants to put tape around the edge of the largest table in the classroom. How much tape will she need? Explain how you got the answer.

2 The perimeter of Pilar's yard is 100 feet. Draw a picture of what her yard might look like, and label each side.

Perimeter Problems

3 Draw three different rectangles below that each have a perimeter of 20 centimeters, and label each side.

Missing Side Lengths

For each shape, find the missing side length.
Show your solution.

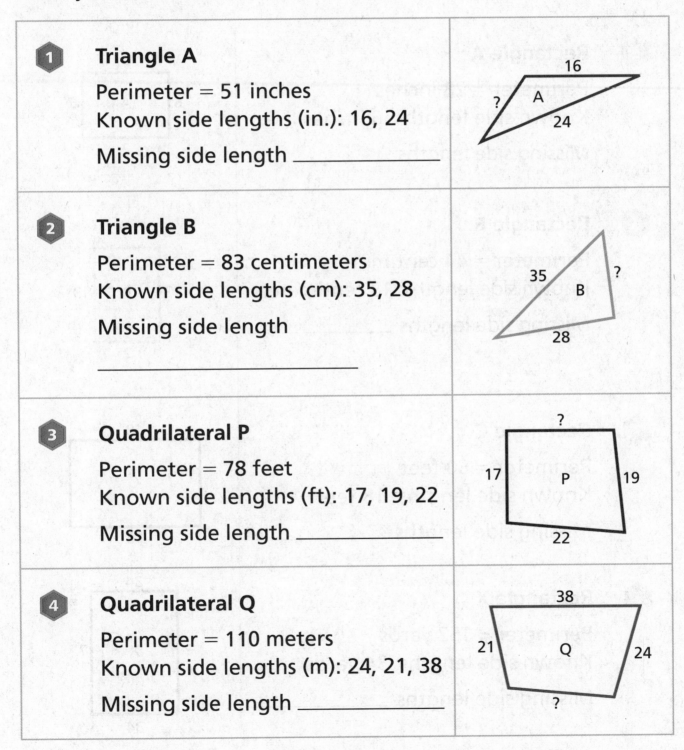

1 **Triangle A**

Perimeter = 51 inches
Known side lengths (in.): 16, 24

Missing side length _____

2 **Triangle B**

Perimeter = 83 centimeters
Known side lengths (cm): 35, 28

Missing side length

_____

3 **Quadrilateral P**

Perimeter = 78 feet
Known side lengths (ft): 17, 19, 22

Missing side length _____

4 **Quadrilateral Q**

Perimeter = 110 meters
Known side lengths (m): 24, 21, 38

Missing side length _____

Missing Side Lengths

For each rectangle, find the missing side lengths.
Show your solution.

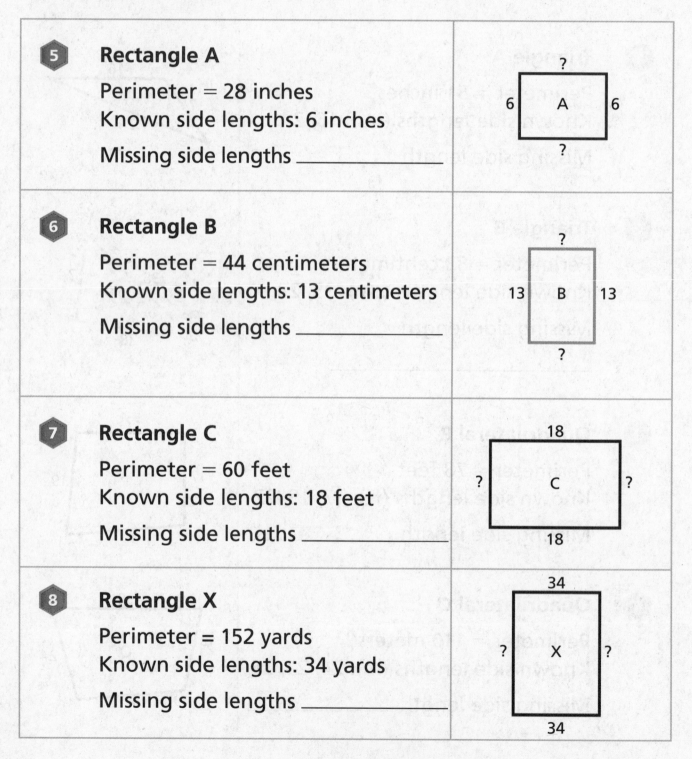

5 Rectangle A

Perimeter = 28 inches
Known side lengths: 6 inches

Missing side lengths _____

6 Rectangle B

Perimeter = 44 centimeters
Known side lengths: 13 centimeters

Missing side lengths _____

7 Rectangle C

Perimeter = 60 feet
Known side lengths: 18 feet

Missing side lengths _____

8 Rectangle X

Perimeter = 152 yards
Known side lengths: 34 yards

Missing side lengths _____

NAME

DATE

Crossing Over 100

Solve the following sets of related problems. How would you use one problem to solve the next one?

1 100 − 54 = _____

110 − 54 = _____

120 − 54 = _____

2 100 − 86 = _____

112 − 86 = _____

132 − 86 = _____

3 100 − 92 = _____

121 − 92 = _____

141 − 92 = _____

4 100 − 37 = _____

110 − 37 = _____

120 − 37 = _____

5 100 − 49 = _____

120 − 49 = _____

124 − 49 = _____

6 100 − 83 = _____

130 − 83 = _____

138 − 83 = _____

NOTE

Students practice solving subtraction problems in related sets.

MWI Subtraction Strategies: Adding Up and Subtracting Back

Ordering Shapes by Perimeter

1 Look at the shapes below. Put them in order from the shortest to the longest perimeter **without** measuring.

_____ _____ _____ _____ _____

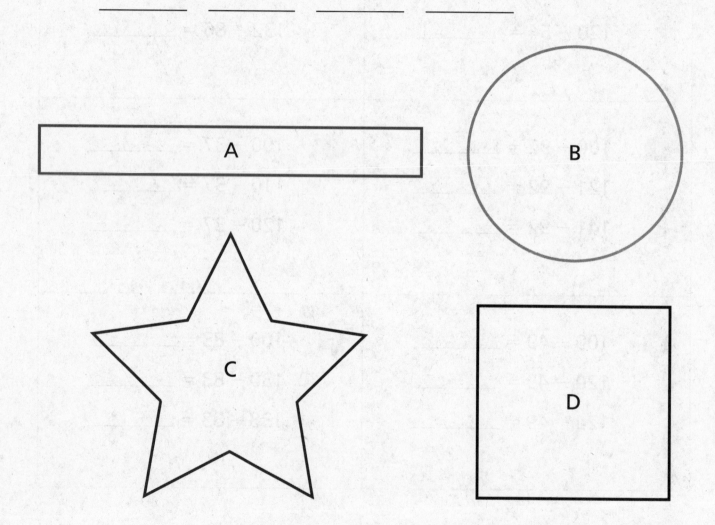

Ordering Shapes by Perimeter

2 Measure the perimeter of each shape to the nearest inch. Put them in order from shortest to longest. Write the perimeter of each shape.

_____

_____

_____

_____

3 Compare the lists you made before and after you measured. Did anything surprise you about the perimeters of these shapes? Explain what you found out.

NAME

DATE

Making Shapes

Draw a sketch of each given shape. Label the length of each side.

1 Square with a perimeter of 80 units

2 Rectangle with a perimeter of 120 units

3 Square with a perimeter of 160 units

4 Rectangle with a perimeter of 180 units

Ongoing Review

5 What is the perimeter of a square with 6-inch sides?

Ⓐ 12 inches   Ⓑ 18 inches   Ⓒ 24 inches   Ⓓ 36 inches

NOTE

Students draw and label shapes with given perimeters.
MWI **Perimeter**

Frog Jumps

Frog A	Frog B	Frog C	Frog D

Start   Finish

27 centimeters   34 centimeters   25 centimeters   28 centimeters

 1 Frogs A, B, C, and D had a jumping relay race. How many centimeters did they jump altogether?

2 Combine the jumps of frogs A and B and the jumps of frogs C and D. Which pair of frogs jumped farther? How much farther?

NOTE

Students practice adding and subtracting centimeters.
MWI **Adding More Than Two Numbers**

© Pearson Education 3

Frog Jumps

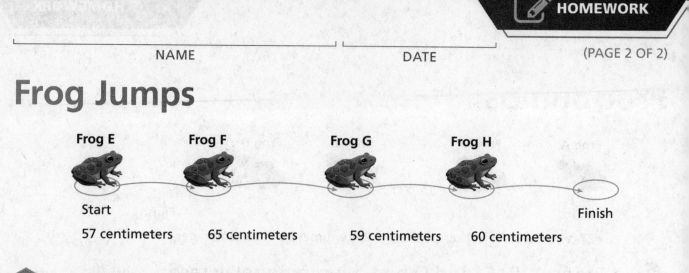

Frog E   **Frog F**   **Frog G**   **Frog H**

Start   Finish

57 centimeters   65 centimeters   59 centimeters   60 centimeters

3   Frogs E, F, G, and H are bullfrogs. How many centimeters did they jump altogether?

4   How much farther did Frogs E, F, G, and H jump than Frogs A, B, C, and D?

NAME   DATE

Building Shapes

Aaron combined two of these shapes to make a new shape.

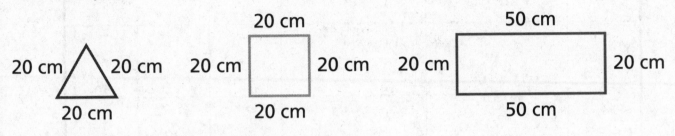

Here is the new shape Aaron made.

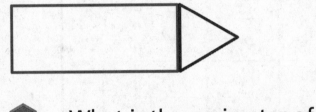

1 What is the perimeter of Aaron's new shape?

_____

2 Combine the rectangle and the square. Draw the new shape. Find the perimeter. _____

3 Combine the square and the triangle. Draw the new shape. Find the perimeter. _____

NOTE

Students combine shapes and find the perimeter of the new shape.
MWI **Solving Perimeter Problems**

© Pearson Education 3

NAME   DATE

10 × 8 Rectangle

The Perfect Cover-Up

1 Choose one of the tetromino shapes. Draw the shape in the first column of the chart on the next page. Use 10–15 of that shape to cover as many squares as you can on the 10 × 8 rectangle on *Student Activity Book* page 232.

2 Do you think this shape will completely cover the whole rectangle? How do you know? Answer this question in the second column of the chart.

3 If you are not sure whether it will cover the entire rectangle, you can do one of the following:

a. Build more of the same tetromino shape and continue to cover the rectangle.

b. On the rectangle, color the tetromino shapes you have already covered. Color all 4 squares in one tetromino shape the same color, but make each tetromino a different color. Then, try to cover the rest of the rectangle by moving the tetromino shapes or by coloring where additional tetrominoes will fit.

4 Answer the questions in the other columns of the chart.

5 Repeat these steps with the other tetromino shapes.

The Perfect Cover-Up

Tetromino Shape	Will it be a "perfect cover-up"? Yes or No	Why or why not?	How many cover the rectangle?

6 Which tetromino shapes were not a "perfect cover-up"? Explain why you think each one did not cover the 10 × 8 rectangle.

How Many More?

Solve the following problems and show your solutions on the number lines provided.

1 $116 +$ _____ $= 250$

2 $94 +$ _____ $= 260$

3 $143 +$ _____ $= 300$

4 $167 +$ _____ $= 325$

NOTE

Students find the missing number to make an addition equation correct.
MWI Subtraction Strategies: Adding Up and Subtracting Back

NAME _____ DATE _____

Addition Starter Problems

Solve each problem two ways, using the first steps listed below. Show your work clearly.

1   138 + 174 = _____

Start by solving 138 + 4.	Start by solving 130 + 170.

2   259 + 163 = _____

Start by solving 200 + 100.	Start by solving 60 + 60.

NAME

DATE

More Missing Side Lengths

For each shape, write an equation or draw a picture to find the missing side lengths. Show your solutions.

1 Triangle D has a perimeter of 64 meters. Two of its side lengths are 32 meters and 16 meters. What is its missing side length?

2 Triangle E has a perimeter of 125 inches. Two of its side lengths are 26 inches and 55 inches. What is its missing side length?

3 Quadrilateral M has a perimeter of 79 yards. Three of its side lengths are 30 yards, 17 yards, and 17 yards. What is its missing side length?

4 Rectangle L has a perimeter of 108 centimeters. Opposite sides of the rectangle have lengths of 27 centimeters each. What are its missing side lengths?

NOTE

Given the perimeter and some side lengths, students find the missing side length.

MWI Solving Perimeter Problems

Tetromino Puzzle

Find the area of each shape.

Tetromino Puzzle

Find the area of each shape.

NAME   DATE

Multiplication Stories

Solve each story problem. Show your work.

1 Eric's dad bought 6 packages of hot dog buns for a cookout. Each package has 8 hot dog buns.

a. How many hot dog buns did he buy? _____

b. If Eric's dad buys two more packages of hot dog buns, what multiplication equation can you solve to find the total number of buns he will have?

_____

2 Mrs. Gordon's flower garden has 7 rows of flowers. There are 9 flowers in each row.

a. How many flowers are in Mrs. Gordon's garden?

_____

b. Mrs. Lee's flower garden has three more rows of 9 flowers than Mrs. Gordon's garden. What multiplication equation can you solve to find how many flowers Mrs. Lee's garden has?

_____

NOTE

Students solve story problems involving multiplication facts.
MWI Solving Multiplication Problems

Rectangle

Finding the Area of Rectangles

Use color tiles to find the area of the rectangles.

1   Area: _____ square inches

2   Area: _____ square inches

3   Area: _____ square inches

Finding the Area of Rectangles

Use color tiles to find the area of the rectangles.

4 Area: _____ square inches

5 Area: _____ square inches

Find the Area

Each rectangle has a perimeter of 12 inches. Find the area.

1 Area: _____ square inches

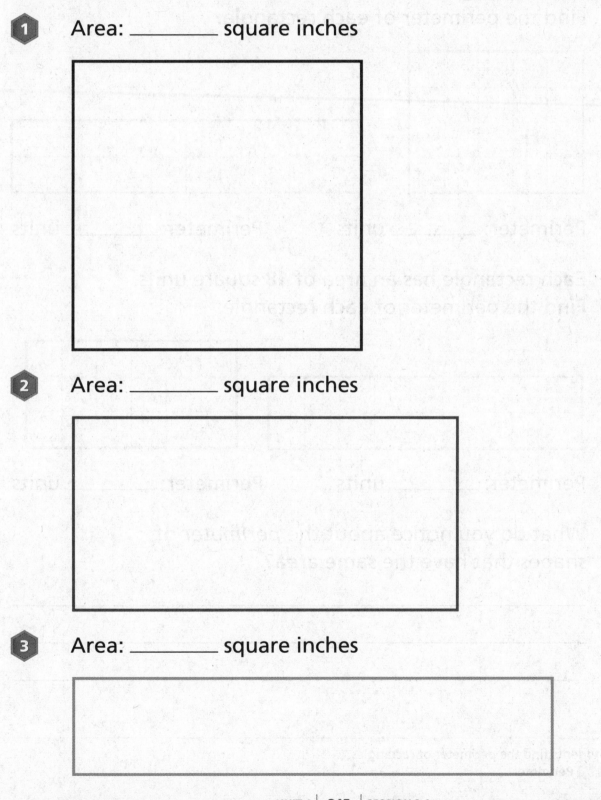

2 Area: _____ square inches

3 Area: _____ square inches

Area and Perimeter

 Each rectangle has an area of 20 square units.
Find the perimeter of each rectangle.

Perimeter: _____ units   Perimeter: _____ units

2 Each rectangle has an area of 18 square units.
Find the perimeter of each rectangle.

Perimeter: _____ units   Perimeter: _____ units

3 What do you notice about the *perimeter* of
shapes that have the same area?

_____

_____

_____

NOTE

Students find the perimeter of rectangles.
MWI **Perimeter**

© Pearson Education 3

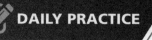
Area and Perimeter

4 Each rectangle has a perimeter of 16 units.
Find the area of each rectangle.

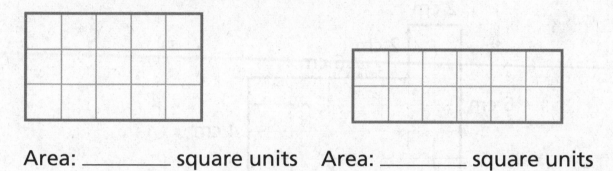

Area: _____ square units   Area: _____ square units

5 Each rectangle has a perimeter of 14 units.
Find the area of each rectangle.

Area: _____ square units   Area: _____ square units

6 What do you notice about the *area* of shapes
that have the same perimeter?

_____

_____

_____

NOTE

Students find the area of rectangles.
MWI Measuring Area With Square Units

Area of Other Shapes

Find the area of each of the shapes below. Show your work, including any equations you used.

1

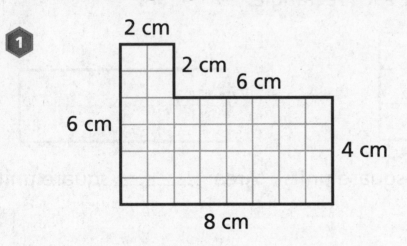

2 cm
2 cm
6 cm
6 cm
4 cm
8 cm

2

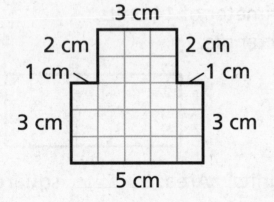

3 cm
2 cm   2 cm
1 cm   1 cm
3 cm   3 cm
5 cm

3

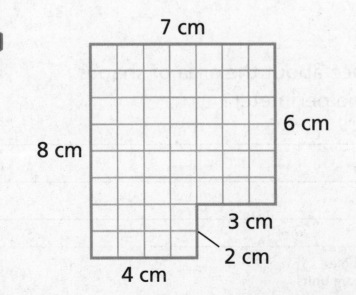

7 cm
6 cm
8 cm
3 cm
2 cm
4 cm

Area of Other Shapes

Find the area of each of the shapes below. Show your work, including any equations you used.

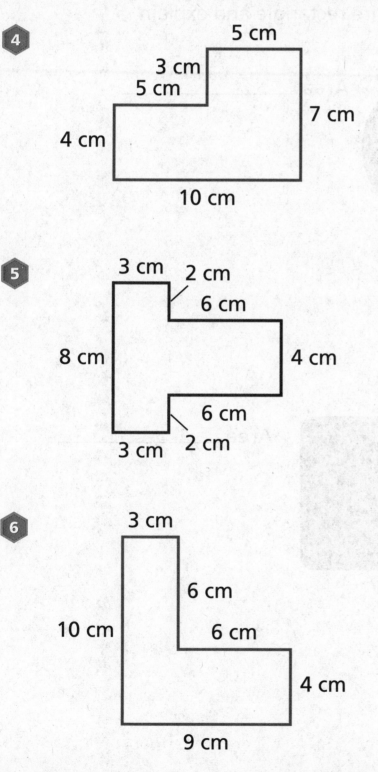

4

5 cm

3 cm

5 cm

7 cm

4 cm

10 cm

5

3 cm   2 cm

6 cm

8 cm   4 cm

6 cm

3 cm   2 cm

6

3 cm

6 cm

10 cm   6 cm

4 cm

9 cm

What's the Area?

The drawings below show different rectangles partially covered by shapes. Determine how many square centimeter tiles are in the entire rectangle and explain how you found your answer.

1
Area _____

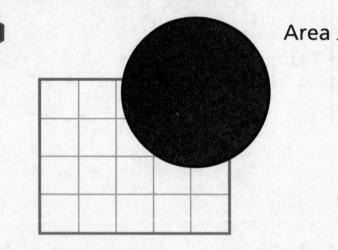

2
Area _____

What's the Area?

Determine how many square centimeter tiles are in the entire rectangle and explain how you found your answer.

3

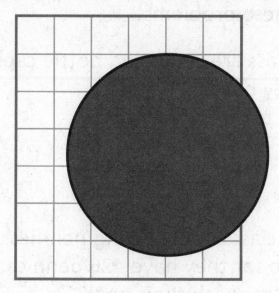

Area _____

4

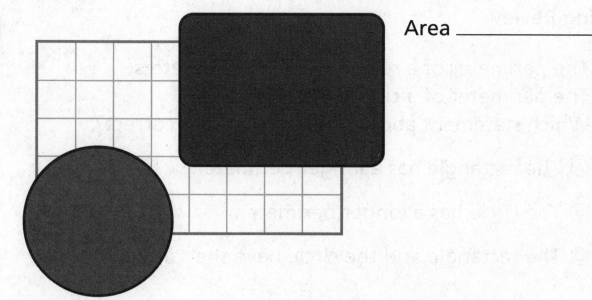

Area _____

NAME _____ DATE _____

Class Collections

For each problem, write an equation, solve the problem, and show your solution. You may use a number line or your 1,000 Chart to help you solve these problems.

1 The students in Ms. Ahmed's class are collecting bottle caps. Their goal is to collect 500. They have 317 so far. How many more do they need to reach their goal?

2 The students in Ms. Kennedy's class are collecting pennies. Their goal is to collect $7.00. So far they have 426 pennies. How many more do they need to reach their goal?

Ongoing Review

3 The perimeter of a rectangle is 39 centimeters.
The perimeter of a circle is 39 meters.
Which statement about the two shapes is correct?

Ⓐ The rectangle has a longer perimeter.

Ⓑ The circle has a longer perimeter.

Ⓒ The rectangle and the circle have the same perimeter.

NOTE
_____

Students find the difference between 3-digit numbers. Ask for explanations on how each problem was solved.
MWI Tools for Solving Subtraction Problems

NAME   DATE

Make Some Frog Jumps

Answer the questions below, and explain how you solved the problem.

1   Three frogs jumped a total of 115 centimeters. How far could each frog have jumped?

Frog 1   Frog 2   Frog 3

_____   _____   _____

How did you solve it?

2   Four frogs jumped a total of 185 centimeters. How far could each frog have jumped?

Frog 1   Frog 2   Frog 3   Frog 4

_____   _____   _____   _____

How did you solve it?

NOTE

Students practice solving addition problems by finding 3 or 4 addends that equal the given sum.

MWI Adding More Than Two Numbers

NAME   DATE

How Big Is Your Foot?

Find the perimeter and area of your foot. Then answer the following questions.

 1 What is the perimeter of your foot?

Describe how you measured the perimeter.

 2 What is the area of your foot?

Explain how you found your answer.

Seven-Unit Shapes

Use the Square and Triangle Cutouts (T35) to make three new shapes with an area of seven square units. Remember that each new shape must, like tetrominoes, have full sides touching.

Tape or glue the new shapes you make on a large piece of paper. You may also draw the new shapes.

1 Use only squares in your first shape.

2 Use only triangles in your second shape.

3 Use both squares and triangles in your third shape.

Ongoing Review

4 What is the area of the blue shape below?

Ⓐ 2 square units

Ⓑ 3 square units

Ⓒ $3\frac{1}{2}$ square units

Ⓓ 4 square units

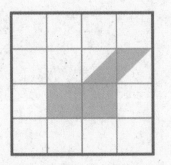

NOTE

Students build shapes with an area of 7 square units.

MWI Measuring Area With Square Units

NAME

DATE

Multiplication Facts Practice

For each expression, write the product and explain how you found the answer.

1 3 × 9 _____

2 6 × 7 _____

3 7 × 8 _____

4 9 × 9 _____

5 5 × 8 _____

NOTE

Students solve multiplication problems.
MWI Learning Multiplication Facts

NAME   DATE

Area of Irregular Shapes

Find the area of each shape. Show your solutions.

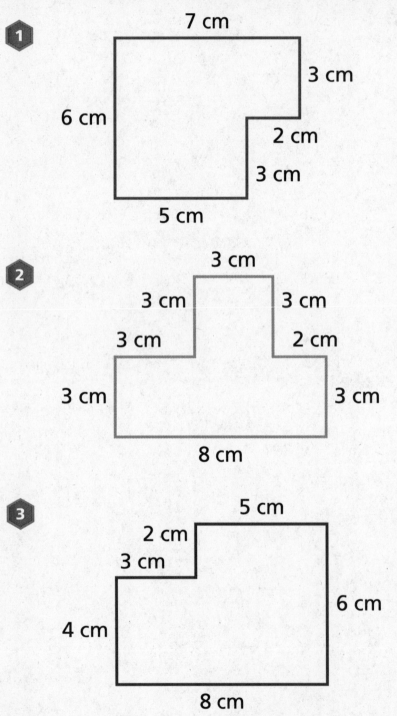

1

7 cm

3 cm

6 cm

2 cm

3 cm

5 cm

2

3 cm

3 cm   3 cm

3 cm   2 cm

3 cm   3 cm

8 cm

3

5 cm

2 cm

3 cm

6 cm

4 cm

8 cm

NOTE

Students find the area of shapes that can be divided into rectangles.
MWI **Area**

Building Triangles

Follow the directions below to make triangles with your straw building kit. Draw a picture of each triangle you make, and label the lengths of the straws you use for each side.

 1 Make a triangle with all sides the same length.

2 Make a triangle from a 3-inch, a 4-inch, and a 5-inch straw.

Building Triangles

 3 Make a triangle with two sides the same length and one side a different length.

 4 Can you find three straws that will not make a triangle? Draw them and label their lengths. Why do you think they will not make a triangle?

Collecting Stickers and Pennies

For each problem, write an equation, solve the problem, and show your solution.

1 Jung collects animal stickers. She has 158 stickers in her collection. On her birthday, her mother gave her 64 more stickers to add to her collection. How many animal stickers does Jung have now?

2 Oscar collects sports stickers. In his sticker box, he has 213 baseball stickers and 189 tennis stickers. How many of these sports stickers does Oscar have altogether?

3 Last month Kim collected 130 pennies. This month she collected 82 pennies. How much money does Kim have now?

4 Gil had 298 pennies in his collection. His younger sister had 112 pennies in her collection. They combined their collections to buy a present for their parents. How much money did they have altogether?

NOTE

Students practice solving addition problems that involve 2- and 3-digit numbers.
MWI **Addition Strategies: Adding One Number in Parts**

NAME

DATE

Is It a Triangle?

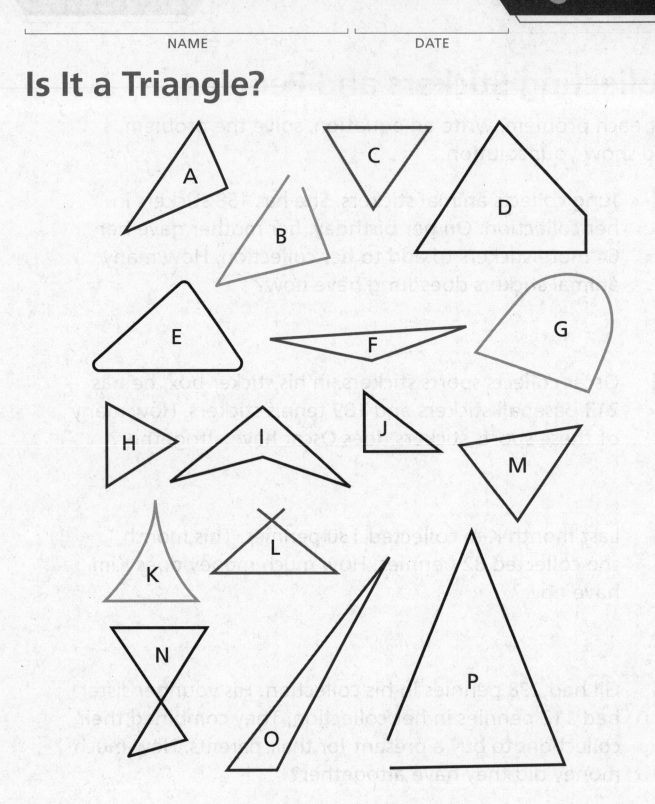

Which Are Triangles?

1 Which of the triangles on page 262 are actually triangles? Without showing your partner, list the letter of each shape in the box below where you think it belongs.

These shapes are triangles:	These shapes are NOT triangles:

2 Now compare your list with your partner's. Discuss any shapes on which you disagree.

3 After you have discussed the triangles with your partner, write why you think certain shapes are triangles and others are not triangles.

Which Are Triangles?

4 Draw some shapes that are triangles and some that are NOT triangles. Then trade this sheet with your partner. Put the letter *T* in each shape your partner drew that is a triangle, and put the letters *NT* in each shape your partner drew that is NOT a triangle.

NAME

DATE

Not a Triangle

Explain why each shape in the table is NOT a triangle.

Shape	This shape is not a triangle because...
Example:	the sides are not closed.
1	
2	
3	
4	

Ongoing Review

5 Which statement about triangles is correct?

Ⓐ Triangles have 4 sides.

Ⓑ Triangles must have a 90-degree angle.

Ⓒ Triangles have 3 vertices.

Ⓓ Triangles must have 3 equal sides.

NOTE

Students use their knowledge of properties of a triangle to explain why a shape is not a triangle.

MWI Triangles

NAME _____ DATE _____

Related Problems

Solve the following sets of related problems. Think about how you can use one problem to solve the next one.

1   250 − 100 = _____

250 − 90 = _____

250 − 95 = _____

250 − 105 = _____

2   280 + _____ = 283

270 + _____ = 283

250 + _____ = 283

220 + _____ = 283

3   53 + 47 = _____

153 + 147 = _____

253 + 147 = _____

253 + 247 = _____

4
$$\begin{array}{r} 400 \\ -\ 25 \\ \hline \end{array} \qquad \begin{array}{r} 401 \\ -\ 25 \\ \hline \end{array} \qquad \begin{array}{r} 401 \\ -\ 26 \\ \hline \end{array}$$

NOTE

Students practice solving addition and subtraction problems in related sets.
MWI Subtraction Strategies: Adding Up and Subtracting Back

Building Quadrilaterals

Follow the directions below to make quadrilaterals with your straw building kit.

 1 Make two different rectangles. Draw them here and label the length of each of the sides.

How are they the same?

_____

How are they different?

_____

2 Make two different squares. Draw them here and label the length of each of the sides.

How are they the same?

_____

How are they different?

_____

Building Quadrilaterals

Follow the directions below to make quadrilaterals with your straw building kit.

 3 Make four different quadrilaterals that are not squares or rectangles. Draw them here and label the length of each of the sides.

How are they the same?

_____

How are they different?

_____

NAME

DATE

How Many Are Left?

For each problem, write an equation, solve the problem, and show your solution.

 1 Keith had 300 animal stickers. He gave 28 tiger stickers to the science teacher. How many stickers did Keith have left?

 2 Jane had 250 mouse stickers. Her cat scratched up 62 stickers. How many stickers did Jane have left?

 3 Ms. Donaldson had 280 teddy bears in her collection. She sold 146 of them to the Children's Museum. How many are left?

 4 Ms. Patel had 134 mystery books in her collection. She sold 65 of them to another collector. How many are left?

NOTE

Students practice solving 2- and 3-digit subtraction problems.
MWI **Subtraction Situations**

© Pearson Education 3

NAME

DATE

Finding Triangles and Quadrilaterals at Home

Find examples of these shapes at home. List or draw them below.

Triangles	Squares
Rectangles	What other quadrilaterals can you find?

NOTE

Students have been using materials to build shapes that have three and four sides and identifying the characteristics of triangles and quadrilaterals. In this homework, they find these shapes in real-life objects.
MWI Polygons

Building More Triangles and Quadrilaterals

Follow the directions below to make triangles and quadrilaterals with your straw building kit. Draw a picture of each shape you make, and label the lengths of the straws you used for each side.

 1 Rhombuses have 4 equal length sides. Make three different rhombuses.

2 Make two different triangles that have all sides the same length.

3 Make a triangle that has a right angle.

 4 Make a triangle that has 3 different side lengths.

Building More Triangles and Quadrilaterals

 5 Make a quadrilateral that has at least one right angle and is not a rectangle.

 6 Make a quadrilateral that has at least one angle that is smaller than a right angle.

 7 Make a quadrilateral that has at least one angle that is larger than a right angle.

8 Find the perimeter of each of the shapes you made out of straws. Record the perimeter of each shape in an equation next to the drawing you did of the shape.

NAME

DATE

Is It a Quadrilateral?

Look at each shape below. For each shape that is **NOT** a quadrilateral, explain why it is not one.

Shape	This shape is NOT a quadrilateral because...
Example:	it has five sides.
1	
2	
3	
4	

Ongoing Review

5 Which statement is **NOT** true?

Ⓐ A right angle is a square corner.

Ⓑ All quadrilaterals have 4 right angles.

Ⓒ A triangle can have a right angle.

Ⓓ All squares have right angles.

NOTE

Students use their knowledge of properties of a quadrilateral to determine whether a shape is a quadrilateral and to explain why a shape is not a quadrilateral.
MWI Quadrilaterals

NAME _____ DATE _____

Make $1.00, Make $2.00

1 Fill in the blanks to make combinations of four amounts that add up to $1.00.

Example:

___25¢___ + ___25¢___ + ___40¢___ + ___10¢___ = ___$1.00___

_____ + ___15¢___ + _____ + _____ = ___$1.00___

_____ + _____ + ___10¢___ + _____ = ___$1.00___

_____ + ___30¢___ + _____ + _____ = ___$1.00___

2 Now fill in the blanks to make combinations of four amounts that add up to $2.00.

_____ + ___35¢___ + _____ + _____ = ___$2.00___

_____ + _____ + ___60¢___ + _____ = ___$2.00___

_____ + _____ + _____ + ___95¢___ = ___$2.00___

NOTE

Students practice finding combinations of amounts that add to a given total.
MWI Adding More Than Two Numbers

NAME

DATE

How Much Taller? How Much Longer?

For each problem, write an equation, solve the problem, and show your solution. You may use number lines or drawings to help you explain your thinking.

1 Mr. Vega is 185 centimeters tall. Oscar is 129 centimeters tall. How much taller is Mr. Vega than Oscar?

2 A basketball player is 216 centimeters tall. How much taller is the basketball player than Mr. Vega?

3 The Burmese python at the Midtown Zoo is 330 centimeters long. The boa constrictor is 217 centimeters long. How much longer is the Burmese python?

NOTE

Students compare heights and lengths in centimeters.
MWI Subtraction Situations

© Pearson Education 3

Cube Patterns, Arrays, and Multiples of 10

Cube Patterns, Arrays, and Multiples of 10

Cube Patterns: Red, Blue, Green

Build a train of 12 cubes with these colors, in this order: red, blue, green, red, blue, green, red, blue, green, red, blue, green.

If this pattern keeps repeating the same colors:

What is the color of the 13th cube? _____

What is the color of the 18th cube? _____

What is the color of the 20th cube? _____

What is the color of the 25th cube? _____

What is the color of the 33rd cube? _____

How did you figure out the color of the 33rd cube?

Adding and Subtracting Multiples of 10 and 100

Solve each set of problems below.

1
$381 - 50 =$ _____
$381 - 70 =$ _____
$381 - 90 =$ _____

2
$239 + 100 =$ _____
$239 + 200 =$ _____
$239 + 400 =$ _____

3
$157 + 40 =$ _____
$157 + 60 =$ _____
$157 + 80 =$ _____

4
$862 - 50 =$ _____
$862 - 150 =$ _____
$862 - 200 =$ _____

Ongoing Review

5 Which number makes the equation true?
Mark the correct answer.

$135 +$ _____ $= 300$

Ⓐ 65　　　Ⓑ 165　　　Ⓒ 175　　　Ⓓ 235

NOTE

Students practice adding and subtracting multiples of 10 and 100.
MWI **Adding and Subtracting Tens and Hundreds**

NAME   DATE

About the Mathematics in This Unit

Dear Family,

Our class is starting a new unit about multiplication and division called *Cube Patterns, Arrays, and Multiples of 10*. During this unit, students build on the work they did in Unit 1. Students identify and analyze arithmetic patterns to examine the relationship between multiplication and division, solve multiplication and division problems, consider what it means to multiply a single-digit number by a multiple of 10, and solve multi-step problems. They also learn the remaining multiplication facts.

Throughout the unit, students work toward these goals:

Benchmarks	Examples
Represent and explain the relationship between multiplication and division.	$4 \times 3 = 12$ $12 \div 3 = 4$ Sarah could split 12 into 4 equal groups which is division. Sarah could make 4 groups of 3 which is multiplication. They're related because they both involve Sarah splitting them into equal groups.
Solve multiplication and division word problems and write equations to represent problems.	There are 45 students from Grade 3 at the Ernest School who are going on a field trip. There are 9 chaperones. How many students will go with each chaperone? $45 \div 9 = \underline{\hspace{2cm}}$
Solve division problems (2-digit number divided by single-digit number).	$42 \div 6 = \underline{\hspace{2cm}}$ $6 \times 6 = 36$ $6 \times 1 = 6$ $36 + 6 = 42$ $6 + 1 = 7$

About the Mathematics in This Unit

Benchmarks	Examples
Demonstrate fluency with multiplication facts to 10 × 10.	7×8 8×7 Start with $\underline{5 \times 8 = 40}$
Multiply a single-digit number by a multiple of 10 (up to 90).	Elena sells marbles in her toy store. Elena orders five 90-packs of marbles from The Toy Factory for her store. How many marbles does she order? $5 \times 90 = 450$
Solve multi-step problems involving multiplication and addition.	Zhang is organizing a birthday celebration. He orders eight 7-packs of balloons and three 90-packs of marbles for the celebration. How many items does he order? $8 \times 7 = 56$ $3 \times 90 = 270$ $56 + 270 = 326$

This unit is the second of three units in Grade 3 that focus on multiplication and division. Later this year, students solve multiplication and division problems with larger numbers and learn their division facts.

In our math class, students spend time discussing problems in depth and are asked to share their reasoning and solutions. It is most important that children accurately and efficiently solve math problems in ways that make sense to them. At home, encourage your child to explain his or her math thinking to you.

Please look for more information and activities about Unit 5 that will be sent home in the coming weeks.

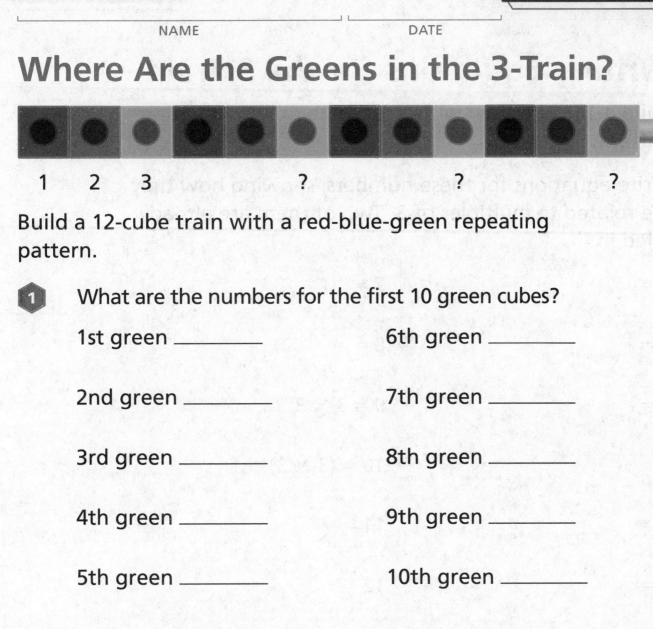

Where Are the Greens in the 3-Train?

NAME _____ DATE _____

1   2   3   ?   ?   ?

Build a 12-cube train with a red-blue-green repeating pattern.

1   What are the numbers for the first 10 green cubes?

1st green _____   6th green _____

2nd green _____   7th green _____

3rd green _____   8th green _____

4th green _____   9th green _____

5th green _____   10th green _____

2   What are you noticing about the numbers that are matched with the green cubes? Why does it work this way?

NAME   DATE

Writing Equations for the 3-Train

Build a 12-cube train with a red-blue-green repeating pattern.

Write equations for these numbers, showing how they are related to multiples of 3. Two of them are already filled in.

1 =   7 =

2 =   8 =

3 = $9 = 3 \times 3$

4 = $10 = (3 \times 3) + 1$

5 =   11 =

6 =   12 =

On a separate piece of paper draw a picture for 8, showing how your equation matches your cube train.

Extra challenge: Can you find a second equation for any of the numbers? It still has to show how the number is related to a multiple of 3.

Where Are the Greens in the 4-Train?

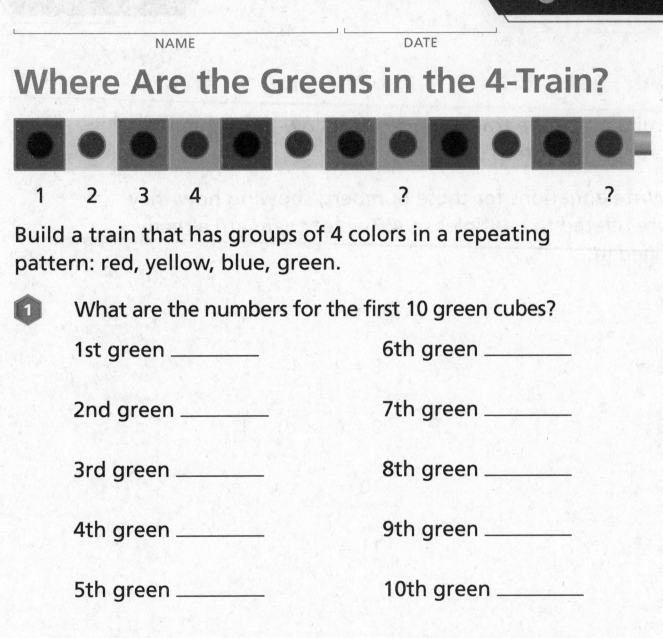

1   2   3   4   ?   ?

Build a train that has groups of 4 colors in a repeating pattern: red, yellow, blue, green.

1   What are the numbers for the first 10 green cubes?

1st green _____   6th green _____

2nd green _____   7th green _____

3rd green _____   8th green _____

4th green _____   9th green _____

5th green _____   10th green _____

2   What are you noticing about the numbers that are matched with the green cubes? Why does it work this way?

Writing Equations for the 4-Train

Build a 12-cube train with a red-yellow-blue-green repeating pattern.

Write equations for these numbers, showing how they are related to multiples of 4. Two of them are already filled in.

1 =   7 =

2 =   8 = 2 × 4

3 =   9 = (2 × 4) + 1

4 =   10 =

5 =   11 =

6 =   12 =

Find two different ways to write an equation for 10 that shows how it is related to a multiple of 4. On a separate piece of paper draw a picture of your cube trains to show why both ways work.

Where Are the Greens in the 6-Train?

1   2   3   4   5   6   ?

Build a train that has groups of 6 colors in a repeating pattern: orange, yellow, white, red, blue, green.

1 What are the numbers for the first 10 green cubes?

1st green _____   6th green _____

2nd green _____   7th green _____

3rd green _____   8th green _____

4th green _____   9th green _____

5th green _____   10th green _____

2 What are you noticing about the numbers that are matched with the green cubes? Why does it work this way?

NAME

DATE

Writing Equations for the 6-Train

Build a 12-cube train with an orange-yellow-white-red-blue-green repeating pattern.

Write equations for these numbers, showing how they are related to multiples of 6. Some of them are already filled in.

1 =   7 = (1 × 6) + 1

2 =   8 = (1 × 6) + 2

3 =   9 =

4 =   10 =

5 =   11 =

6 = 1 × 6   12 =

Draw a picture showing how your equation for 10 matches your cube train. Can you find more than one equation for 10?

NAME _____   DATE _____

More Finding the Area of Rectangles

Use color tiles to find the area of the rectangles.

1 Area: _____ square inches

2 Area: _____ square inches

NOTE

Students practice finding the area of rectangles.
MWI **Measuring Area With Square Units**

© Pearson Education 3

NAME

DATE

Greens in the 5-Train

1 2 3 4 5 ?

1 What are the numbers for the first 10 green cubes?

1st green _____   6th green _____

2nd green _____   7th green _____

3rd green _____   8th green _____

4th green _____   9th green _____

5th green _____   10th green _____

2 What are you noticing about the numbers that are matched with the green cubes? Why does it work this way?

NOTE

Students work on multiplication as they determine the color of cubes associated with particular numbers.
MWI Cube Train Patterns

© Pearson Education 3

NAME

DATE

Addition and Subtraction Problems

Write an equation for each story problem. Solve the problem and show how you solved it.

 1 Roberto has 296 baseball cards. Edwin has 205 football cards. How many sports cards do they have altogether?

 2 Sandra has saved 247 dollars. She spends 150 dollars on new clothes. How much money does she have left?

Solve the problems. Think about how solving one problem in each set can help you solve the others.

3 $158 + 200 = \underline{\hspace{2cm}}$

$158 + 250 = \underline{\hspace{2cm}}$

$258 + 250 = \underline{\hspace{2cm}}$

4 $234 - 130 = \underline{\hspace{2cm}}$

$284 - 130 = \underline{\hspace{2cm}}$

$234 - 140 = \underline{\hspace{2cm}}$

NOTE

Students solve addition and subtraction problems with 3-digit numbers.
MWI **Subtraction Strategies: Adding Up and Subtracting Back**

NAME   DATE

Related Activities to Try at Home

Dear Family,

The activities described here are related to the mathematics in Unit 5. Use the activities below to enrich your child's learning experience.

Multiplication and Division Problems in Everyday Situations
At school, students are solving multiplication and division word problems. Encourage your child to help you solve multiplication and division situations that come up in your daily activities.

- How many legs are on the six dogs we saw in the park?
- How many toes are on eight people?
- I baked a batch of 48 cookies for the bake sale. I need to put them into bags of 6. How many bags can I fill with 6 cookies? Will any be left?
- There are 72 players who will play baseball in teams of 9. How many teams can they make?"

Learning Multiplication Facts Students are expected to know all of the multiplication facts up to 10×10 by the end of Grade 3. They began this work in Unit 1 and will continue to practice the multiplication facts during this unit. You can help your child practice by using the Multiplication Cards they have prepared at school.

How Did You Solve That? Ask your child to tell you about how he or she is multiplying and dividing. Show that you are interested in these approaches. Because these strategies may be unfamiliar to you, listen carefully to your child's explanation; you might even try to do a problem or two, using the new procedure. Let your child be the teacher!

How Are Multiplication and Division Related?

Sarah said, "I can use my cube train to show multiplication and division."

Is she right? Make a 3-train with 12 cubes (red-blue-green repeating pattern) and show how this is true. Explain your idea to someone else.

Then draw a picture to show what you mean. Explain your idea in writing and with equations so that someone else can understand your picture.

Does the same thing work for a 4-train or a 6-train? If you have time, try to prove your idea with a 4-train or a 6-train. Draw a picture and explain your idea in writing and with equations.

NAME _____ DATE _____

How Many Days?

Solve the story problems below. Write a multiplication equation for each problem and show how you solved it.

There are 7 days in a week.

1   How many days are in 3 weeks? _____

     Sample Equation: $3 \times 7 =$ _____

2   How many days are in 5 weeks? _____

     Equation: _____

3   How many days are in 7 weeks? _____

     Equation: _____

Ongoing Review

4   Which number has 26 tens? Mark the correct answer.

     Ⓐ 26   Ⓑ 126   Ⓒ 226   Ⓓ 260

NOTE

Students practice multiplication by solving story problems.
MWI **Solving Multiplication Problems**

NAME   DATE

Counting Around the Class

1 Mr. Brown's class counted by 4s. The 1st person said 4, the 2nd said 8, and the 3rd said 12. How many people counted to get to 36? How do you know?

2 Ms. Wilson's class counted by 6s. The 1st person said 6, the 2nd said 12, and the 3rd said 18.

   a. What number did the 6th person say? How do you know?

   b. What number did the 12th person say? How do you know?

3 Ms. Ross's class counted by 5s. The 1st person said 5, the 2nd said 10, and the 3rd said 15.

   a. How many people counted to get to 100? How do you know?

   b. When Ms. Ross's class was counting by 5s, did anyone say the number 72? How do you know?

NOTE

Students find the multiples of a given number and solve multiplication problems.
MWI Skip Counting

NAME _____ DATE _____

How Much Taller?

For each problem, write an equation, solve the problem, and show your solution.

Average Giraffe Heights

Female Adult: 168 inches   Baby: 72 inches   Male Adult: 216 inches

1 How much taller is a female giraffe than a baby giraffe?

2 How much taller is a male giraffe than a female giraffe?

3 How much taller is a male giraffe than a baby giraffe?

NOTE

Students use addition and/or subtraction to compare two different heights.
MWI Subtraction Situations

Rounding to 10s and 100s

For each problem, write the number in expanded form, and then round to the nearest ten and hundred.

 432

Expanded form: _____

What is 432 rounded to the nearest ten? _____

What is 432 rounded to the nearest hundred? _____

 903

Expanded form: _____

What is 903 rounded to the nearest ten? _____

What is 903 rounded to the nearest hundred? _____

3 **777**

Expanded form: _____

What is 777 rounded to the nearest ten? _____

What is 777 rounded to the nearest hundred? _____

NOTE

Students round whole numbers to the nearest ten and hundred.
MWI Rounding Whole 3-Digit Numbers

NAME _____ DATE _____

Solving Multiplication Problems

Solve the problems below and show how you solved them. For the story problems, also write an equation for the problem.

 1 $6 \times 7 =$ _____

 2 Markers come in sets of 8. Mr. Thompson has 5 sets in his classroom. How many markers does he have in all?

 3 Folders come in packs of 12. Mr. Thompson orders 3 packs. How many folders does he order?

 4
$$\begin{array}{r} 9 \\ \times\, 4 \\ \hline \end{array}$$

NOTE

Students practice solving multiplication problems.
MWI Solving Multiplication Problems

NAME

DATE

Practicing with Multiplication Cards

Help me practice with my Multiplication Cards.

I have the following items:

○ A copy of the directions
○ My Multiplication Cards from school or
6 sheets to make new ones

Here are the front and back of one Multiplication Card:

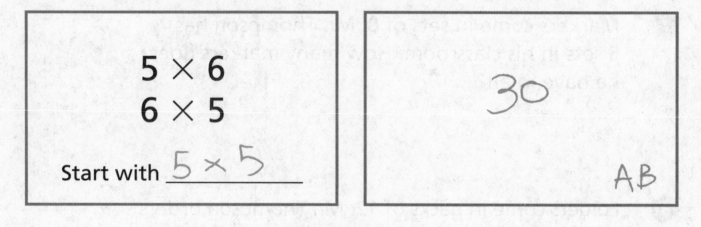

5 × 6
6 × 5

Start with _5 × 5_

30

AB

Related Multiplication Problems

Write an equation for each problem.
Then solve the problem.

Set A

Ms. Smith packs boxes of toy cars in a factory that
makes toy cars and sells them to toy stores. She puts
7 cars in each box. On Monday she packed 4 boxes of
cars to send to the Jump Toy Store. How many cars did
she pack?

On Wednesday, the Play All Day Toy Store ordered
8 boxes of toy cars. How many cars did Ms. Smith pack
for the Play All Day Toy Store?

Use a picture or a diagram to show what you notice
about how these two problems are related.

Related Multiplication Problems

Set B

Lynn bought 3 packs of juice boxes. There are 8 juice boxes in each pack. How many juice boxes did she buy?

Mike bought 6 packs of juice boxes. There are 8 juice boxes in each pack. How many juice boxes did he buy?

Related Multiplication Problems

Set C

Mr. Samuel is putting flowers in small vases. He puts
4 flowers in each vase. He fills 9 small vases with flowers.
How many flowers did he put in the vases?

Mr. Samuel is putting flowers in large vases.
He puts 8 flowers in each vase. He fills 9 large vases with
flowers. How many flowers did he put in the vases?

Use a picture or a diagram to show what you notice
about how these two problems are related.

Related Multiplication Problems

Set D

Ms. Brooks was putting together bags of crayons for her students. She put 9 crayons in each bag. She made 3 bags of crayons. How many crayons did she put in the bags?

Another day, Ms. Brooks was making bags of colored pencils for her students. She put 9 colored pencils in each bag. She made 6 bags of colored pencils. How many colored pencils did she put in the bags?

NAME

DATE

School Supplies

Solve each word problem. Show your solutions.

 1 A box of glue sticks has 12 sticks in it.
How many glue sticks are in 3 boxes?

 2 A package of crayons has 8 crayons in it.
How many crayons are in 5 packages?

 3 A bag of erasers has 9 erasers in it.
How many erasers are in 4 bags?

Ongoing Review

4 What is the area of a square with sides that are
7 inches? Mark the correct answer.

Ⓐ 14 square inches   Ⓒ 28 square inches

Ⓑ 47 square inches   Ⓓ 49 square inches

NOTE

Students practice solving multiplication problems in story problem contexts.
MWI Solving Multiplication Problems

More Related Problems

Write an equation for each problem. Solve each problem and show how you solved it.

Set A

There are 4 cars parked in a parking lot. How many wheels are there?

There are 8 cars parked in a parking lot. How many wheels are there?

Set B

Sam made small muffins and large muffins for a bake sale and put them in bags. He fit 3 large muffins in a bag. He made 7 bags of large muffins. How many large muffins did he make?

Sam fit 6 small muffins in a bag. He made 7 bags of small muffins. How many small muffins did he make?

NOTE

Students solve related sets of multiplication problems.
MWI Related Multiplication Problems

More Related Problems

Solve each problem.

Set C

$3 \times 6 =$ _____

$6 \times 6 =$ _____

Choose one set (A, B, or C) and explain how the first problem could help you solve the second problem.

NAME _____ DATE _____

Missing Factor Problems

Find the missing factors. If you used a "start with" fact to solve, write it under the matching problem.

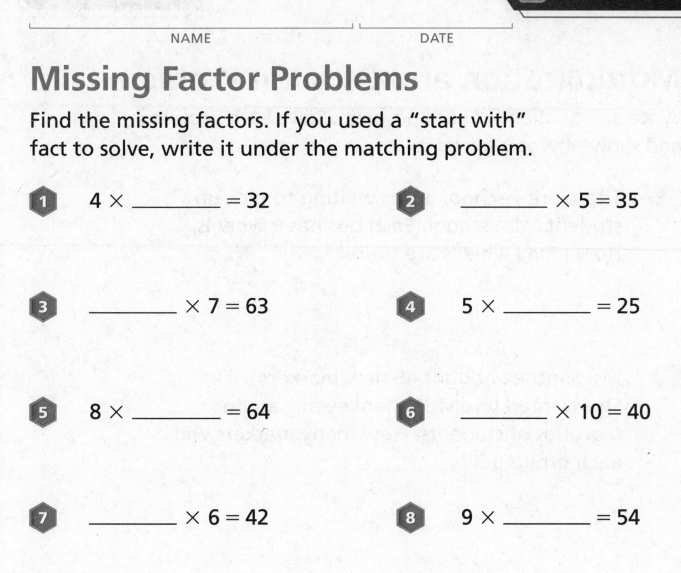

1 $4 \times$ _____ $= 32$

2 _____ $\times 5 = 35$

3 _____ $\times 7 = 63$

4 $5 \times$ _____ $= 25$

5 $8 \times$ _____ $= 64$

6 _____ $\times 10 = 40$

7 _____ $\times 6 = 42$

8 $9 \times$ _____ $= 54$

Ongoing Review

9 Which of the expressions are equal to 300? Mark the **three** correct answers.

☐ $227 + 73$ ☐ $139 + 151$

☐ $34 + 267$ ☐ $96 + 204$

☐ $215 + 85$ ☐ $122 + 168$

NOTE

Students solve problems with missing factors.
MWI Learning Multiplication Facts

Multiplication and Division Problems

Write an equation for each problem. Solve each problem and show how you solved it.

1 There are 7 school buses waiting to pick up students at a school. Each bus has 6 wheels. How many wheels are there?

2 Ms. Sanchez bought 48 new markers. She wanted to divide them evenly among 6 groups of students. How many markers will each group get?

3 The Healthy Grocery Store is selling oranges in bags of 9. Jeremy buys 9 bags. How many oranges did he buy?

4 Stamps come in books of 10. Carla wants to buy 70 stamps. How many books of stamps does she need to buy?

Multiplication and Division Problems

5 There are 45 students in Grade 3 at the Ernest School who are going on a field trip. There are 9 chaperones. How many students will go with each chaperone?

6 Insects have 6 legs. There were 6 insects in a garden. How many legs were there?

Solve each problem.

7 $8 \times 8 = $ _____

8 $7 \times$ _____ $= 56$

NAME   DATE

Add and Subtract

Solve each problem and show how you solved it.

 Garret read 97 pages of a book on Saturday and 113 more pages on Sunday. There are 306 pages in the book. How many pages does he have left to read to finish the book?

 Karen has 445 stickers in her collection. There are 221 animal stickers and 174 cartoon stickers. She also has some flower stickers. How many flower stickers does she have?

3 The fastest time for completing an obstacle course is 218 seconds. Artest completed the first half of the course in 95 seconds. It took him 124 seconds to finish the second half.

a. What is Artest's total time?

b. How does his time compare to the fastest time?

NOTE

Students solve multi-step problems that involve addition and subtraction.
MWI Solving a Multi-Step Problem

NAME   DATE

More Multiplication and Division Problems

Solve each problem. Show how you solved the problem.

 Sam planted tomato plants in his garden. He has 9 rows of tomato plants. He planted 6 tomato plants in each row. How many tomato plants are in Sam's garden?

 $72 \div 8 =$ _____

 Chantelle bought 36 small toys to give out at her birthday party. She invited 9 friends to her party and wants to give them each the same number of toys. How many toys can she give to each friend?

4   $9 \times 9 =$ _____

NOTE

Students solve multiplication and division problems.
MWI Solving Division Problems

A Bake Sale

Write an equation for each story problem.
Solve each problem and show how you solved it.

1 Zhang made 48 muffins for the bake sale. He can fit 8 muffins in a box. How many boxes does he need for all of his muffins?

2 Gina baked 4 sheets of cookies. On each sheet were 12 cookies. How many cookies did she bake?

3 Casawn baked 3 cakes. He sliced each cake into 9 pieces. How many pieces of cake are there in all?

4 Jane baked 36 dinner rolls. She put 6 rolls in each bag. How many bags did she fill?

NOTE

Students solve multiplication and division problems in story contexts.
MWI Solving Division Problems

The Toy Factory

Use the information on The Toy Factory (T51) to answer these questions. Show how you solved each problem. Write an equation that shows the problem and solution. As you work, think about what patterns you notice.

1   **a.** Edwin is having a party. He orders eight 1-packs of jump ropes to give out at his party. How many jump ropes does he order?

   b. Ms. Diaz buys eight 10-packs of jump ropes for her gym class from The Toy Factory. How many jump ropes does she buy?

2   **a.** Keisha orders two 6-packs of toy animals for her pretend farm. How many animals does she order?

   b. Mr. Simmons needs more toy animals for his preschool classroom. He orders two 60-packs of toy animals. How many animals does he order?

The Toy Factory

3
a. Jung is doing an art project. She orders four 5-packs of ink stamps for her art project. How many ink stamps does she order?

b. Mr. Smith orders four 50-packs of ink stamps. How many ink stamps does he order?

4
a. Murphy collects spinning tops. He receives seven 3-packs of spinning tops from The Toy Factory. How many spinning tops does he receive?

b. Becky buys seven 30-packs of spinning tops for a spinning tops contest. How many spinning tops does she buy?

The Toy Factory

5   **a.** Adam loves to play marbles with his friends.
He orders five 9-packs of marbles for his friends
and himself. How many marbles does he order?

b. Elena sells marbles in her toy store. Elena orders
five 90-packs of marbles from The Toy Factory for
her store. How many marbles does she order?

6   Look at your equations. What patterns do you notice?

7   What rule do you think you could use to solve problems
like 7 × 30 or 5 × 90?

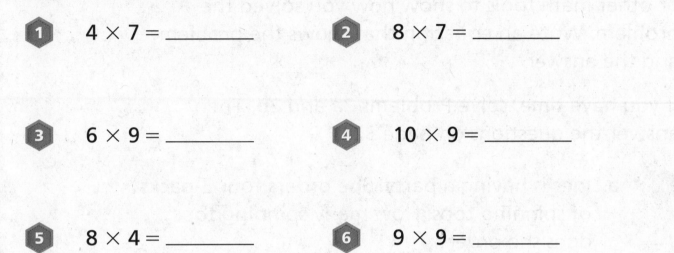
Multiplication Facts

Find each product.

1 $4 \times 7 =$ _____

2 $8 \times 7 =$ _____

3 $6 \times 9 =$ _____

4 $10 \times 9 =$ _____

5 $8 \times 4 =$ _____

6 $9 \times 9 =$ _____

7 $4 \times 9 =$ _____

8 $9 \times 8 =$ _____

9 $7 \times 7 =$ _____

10 $8 \times 10 =$ _____

Ongoing Review

11 Which equation is NOT true?

Ⓐ $143 + 68 = 211$

Ⓒ $126 + 239 = 396$

Ⓑ $177 + 131 = 308$

Ⓓ $182 + 17 = 199$

NOTE

Students practice multiplication facts.
MWI Learning Multiplication Facts

What's the Rule?

Solve each problem. Use cubes, grid paper, drawings, or other math tools to show how you solved the problem. Write an equation that shows the problem and the answer.

If you have time, solve Problems 2a and 2b. Then answer the questions on page 324.

a. Ines is having a party. She orders four 3-packs of spinning tops. How many spinning tops does she order?

b. Oscar orders toys for his school store. He orders four 30-packs of spinning tops. How many spinning tops does he order?

What's the Rule?

2 **a.** Nicholas orders eight 2-packs of whistles.
How many whistles does he get?

b. Jane orders eight 20-packs of whistles.
How many whistles does she get?

What's the Rule?

 3 Look at your representations for Problems 1a and 1b. What do you notice?

 4 How can 4 × 3 help to solve 4 × 30? How does your representation show why that happens?

More Areas of Rectangles

Find the area of each rectangle.

1

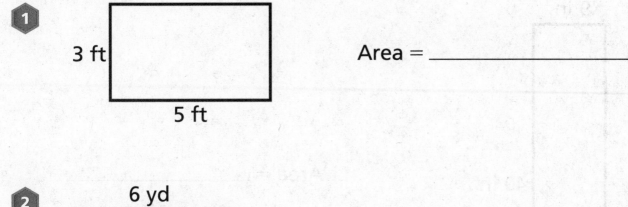

3 ft

5 ft

Area = _____

2

6 yd

9 yd

Area = _____

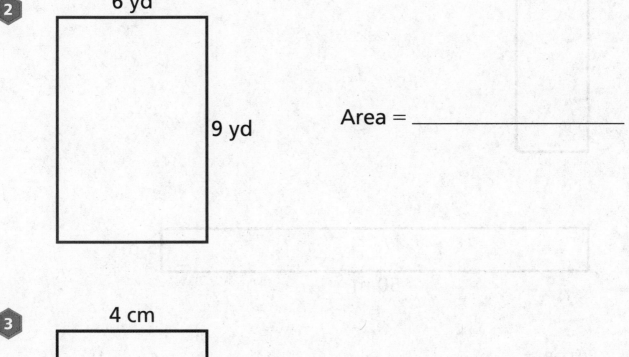

3

4 cm

4 cm

Area = _____

More Areas of Rectangles

Find the area of each rectangle.

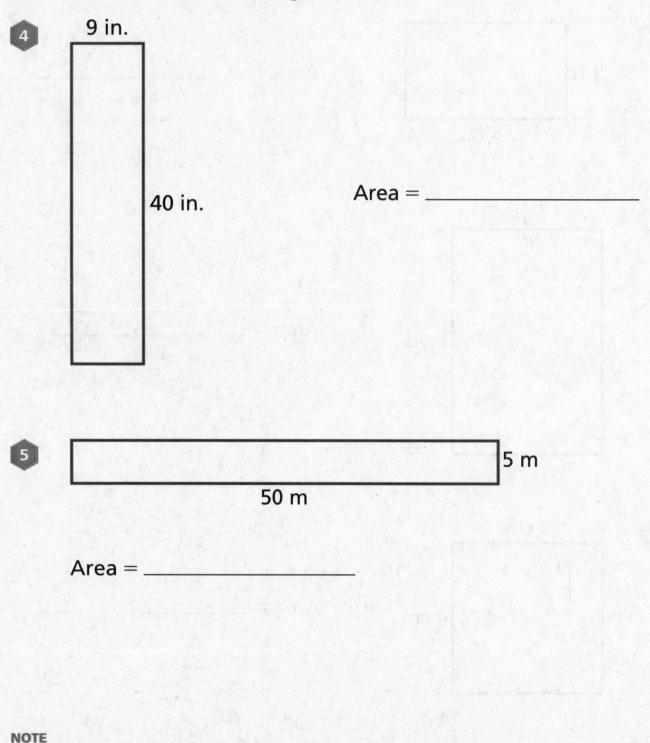

4

9 in.

40 in.

Area = _____

5

5 m

50 m

Area = _____

NOTE

Students find the area of rectangles.
MWI **Area**

UNIT 5 | **326** | SESSION 3.2

© Pearson Education 3

Related Multiplication Problems

Solve the following related multiplication problems.

Explain how you can use one problem to solve the next one.

1 $3 \times 4 =$ _____

$6 \times 4 =$ _____

2 $7 \times 3 =$ _____

$7 \times 6 =$ _____

3 $6 \times 3 =$ _____

$9 \times 3 =$ _____

4 $5 \times 4 =$ _____

$5 \times 8 =$ _____

5 $8 \times 5 =$ _____

$8 \times 7 =$ _____

6 $2 \times 8 =$ _____

$3 \times 8 =$ _____

$4 \times 8 =$ _____

NOTE

Students practice multiplication facts in related sets.
MWI Related Multiplication Problems

© Pearson Education 3

Related Multiplication Problems

7 $2 \times 9 =$ _____

$4 \times 9 =$ _____

8 $3 \times 5 =$ _____

$3 \times 10 =$ _____

9 $2 \times 6 =$ _____

$4 \times 6 =$ _____

$6 \times 6 =$ _____

10 $4 \times 3 =$ _____

$4 \times 6 =$ _____

$4 \times 9 =$ _____

NOTE

Students practice multiplication facts in related sets.
MWI Doubling One Factor

Ordering Different Toys

Write an equation for each problem with a letter standing for the unknown. Solve the problems. Show your work.

1 Arthur orders eight 70-packs of balloons and two 9-packs of marbles for his party store. How many items does he order from The Toy Factory?

2 Ines receives six 80-packs of toy people and eight 9-packs of marbles from The Toy Factory. How many toys did she receive?

3 Denzel orders seven 40-packs of toy cars for a show and nine 6-packs of toy animals for his children. How many toys does he order from The Toy Factory?

4 Zhang is organizing a birthday party. He orders eight 7-packs of balloons and three 90-packs of marbles for the party. How many items does he order?

Ordering Different Toys

 5 Oscar received seven 9-packs of marbles and eight 60-packs of toy animals from The Toy Factory. How many toys did he receive?

 6 Ms. Sanchez orders three 60-packs of toy animals and seven 50-packs of ink stamps for her classroom. How many items did she order?

 7 Deondra is making a piñata for her party. She buys nine 90-packs of marbles and four 60-packs of toy animals to put in the piñata. How many toys does she buy?

8 Kim is organizing a parade. She orders 5 packs of 20 whistles for people to play in the parade and six 30-packs of spinning tops to give away. How many items does she order from The Toy Factory?

NAME   DATE

More Multiplication Facts

Find each product.

1 $6 \times 6 =$ _____

2 $7 \times 8 =$ _____

3 $10 \times 10 =$ _____

4 $6 \times 10 =$ _____

5 $8 \times 6 =$ _____

6 $9 \times 7 =$ _____

7 $6 \times 9 =$ _____

8 $4 \times 6 =$ _____

9 $7 \times 4 =$ _____

10 $10 \times 11 =$ _____

Ongoing Review

11 Which expression is greater than 100?

Ⓐ $322 - 158$ Ⓒ $357 - 279$

Ⓑ $231 - 147$ Ⓓ $274 - 186$

NOTE

Students practice multiplication facts.
MWI **Learning Multiplication Facts**

NAME _____ DATE _____

More Toy Factory Problems

Write an equation for each problem. Solve each problem and show your work.

 1 Party Plaza ordered nine 70-packs of balloons from The Toy Factory. How many balloons did Party Plaza order?

 2 The Toy Factory sometimes does special orders. Mr. Jenkins ordered seven 20-packs of whistles with the Tesla Academy logo on them. How many custom whistles did he order?

3 Abel ordered five 90-packs of marbles to make a marble sculpture. How many marbles did he order?

NOTE

Students multiply single-digit numbers by multiples of 10.

MWI **Multiplying Groups of 10**

© Pearson Education 3

Division Problems

Solve each of the problems below. Show your solution clearly and write an equation. Use a representation to show your solution is correct for at least 2 of the problems.

1 Mr. James bought 42 toy animals for his students to use to count and sort. How many 6-packs did he buy?

2 Jung bought 40 ink stamps to give out at her birthday party. How many 5-packs did she buy?

3 Gil loves toy cars. He saved enough money to buy 32 toy cars. How many 4-packs of toy cars did he get?

4 Beatriz is really good at making balloon animals. She just ordered 35 balloons. How many 7-packs is that?

Division Problems

 5   Zhang needed to get balloons for the school store. 63 balloons were delivered. How many 7-packs of balloons did Zhang order?

 6   Murphy bought her little sister 40 toy people to use when she plays with her toy house and school. How many 8-packs did she buy?

7   Ms. Lee bought 64 toy people for her kindergarten class. How many 8-packs did she buy?

 8   Ines is in charge of decorations for the dance. She ordered 56 balloons. How many 7-packs did she order?

NAME   DATE

More Multiplying by Multiples of 10

Write an equation for each problem. Solve each problem and show how you solved it.

1 Erin's grandmother collects buttons in bags of 30 buttons. She has 9 bags of buttons. How many buttons are there in all?

2 Ms. Altimara has greeting cards in 6 shoeboxes. Each shoebox has 50 greeting cards. How many cards does she have?

3 Enrico's stamp album has 60 pages. There are 8 stamps displayed on each page. How many stamps are in Enrico's album?

Ongoing Review

4 Which factor makes the equation true? Mark the correct answer.

$8 \times (9 \times \underline{\hspace{1.5cm}}) = 720$

Ⓐ 9   Ⓑ 10   Ⓒ 80   Ⓓ 90

NOTE

Students multiply single-digit numbers by multiples of 10.
MWI Multiplying Groups of 10

NAME

DATE

Dividing at the Toy Factory

Write an equation for each problem. Solve each problem and show how you solved it.

1 A carnival ordered 54 toy animals from The Toy Factory. How many 6-packs did the carnival order?

2 Annabelle bought 32 toy people to make a tiny town display. How many 8-packs of toy people did she buy?

3 The gym teacher ordered 90 new jump ropes from The Toy Factory. How many 10-packs did she order?

NOTE

Students solve division problems in a toy-factory context.
MWI Solving Division Problems

Which Toy? How Many?

Keisha wants to order 48 of the same toy. What toy could she order? How many and what size packs of that toy?

Show all your work and how you found the answers. Write an equation (or equations) to represent your solution. Find as many different solutions as you can.

Multi-Step Problems

Write an equation for each problem with a letter standing for the unknown. Solve each problem and show how you solved it.

1 Rory bought seven 3-packs of golf balls and five 20-packs of golf tees. How many golf items did he buy in all?

2 Cho works at the Ice Cream Shoppe. She orders six 50-packs of plastic spoons and four 70-packs of tall cups. How many items did she order in all?

3 Madison Elementary is having a fun fair. The organizers buy nine 40-packs of toy cars and six 60-packs of toy animals for prizes. How many toys did they get for prizes?

NOTE

Students solve multi-step problems that involve multiplication and addition.
MWI Solving a Multi-Step Problem

More Division Problems

Write an equation for each problem. Solve the problem and show how you solved it.

1 Morgan has 81 collectible action figures. He wants to display them equally on 9 shelves in his room. How many action figures should he put on each shelf?

2 Gina made 6 equal batches of cookies. She has a total of 48 cookies. How many cookies were in each batch?

Fill in the blank to solve each problem.

3 $49 \div \underline{\hspace{1.5cm}} = 7$

4 $\underline{\hspace{1.5cm}} \div 8 = 10$

5 $45 \div 5 = \underline{\hspace{1.5cm}}$

6 $7 = 56 \div \underline{\hspace{1.5cm}}$

7 $60 \div \underline{\hspace{1.5cm}} = 10$

8 $\underline{\hspace{1.5cm}} \div 8 = 9$

NOTE

Students solve division problems.
MWI Solving Division Problems

Fair Shares and Fractions on Number Lines

Fair Shares and Fractions on Number Lines

Sharing One Brownie

Cut up large brownie rectangles and glue the pieces below. Show how you would make fair shares.

 2 people share a brownie equally. Each person gets _____.

 4 people share a brownie equally. Each person gets _____.

3 8 people share a brownie equally. Each person gets _____.

ACTIVITY

Sharing One Brownie

4   3 people share a brownie equally. Each person gets _____.

5   6 people share a brownie equally. Each person gets _____.

More Multi-Step Problems

Write an equation for each problem. Solve the problems. Show how you solved each one.

 1 Felicia orders six 70-packs of balloons and four 9-packs of marbles for a fun fair. How many items does she order?

 2 Graham receives seven 80-packs of toy people and nine 9-packs of marbles. How many items did he receive?

NOTE

Students practice solving multi-step problems that involve multiplication and addition.
MWI Solving a Multi-Step Problem

More Multi-Step Problems

3 Dennis orders five 40-packs of toy cars and eight 6-packs of toy animals. How many toys does he order?

4 Tania is planning a party. She orders nine 7-packs of balloons and seven 50-packs of ink stamps. How many items does she order?

About the Mathematics in This Unit

Dear Family,

Our class is starting a new mathematics unit about fractions called *Fair Shares and Fractions on Number Lines*. In this unit, students investigate the meaning of fractions and the ways fractions can be represented. They solve sharing problems (How can 2 people share 3 brownies equally?), represent fractions with area models and on number lines, compare fractions, and determine fraction equivalents $\left(\frac{2}{3} = \frac{4}{6}\right)$.

Throughout the unit, students work toward these goals:

Benchmark/Goal	Examples
1. Partition a quantity into equal parts, and name those parts as fractions or mixed numbers.	$\frac{1}{4}$ $\frac{1}{4}$ $\frac{1}{4}$ $\frac{1}{4}$
2. Represent fractions as numbers on a number line.	Place the following fractions on the number line below: $\frac{3}{4}$, $\frac{9}{8}$. ⟵ 0 $\frac{3}{4}$ 1 $\frac{9}{8}$ 2 3 ⟶
3. Compare fractions with the same numerator or same denominator by reasoning about their size.	Which is greater $\frac{2}{3}$ or $\frac{2}{4}$? $\frac{2}{3} > \frac{2}{4}$ because $\frac{2}{4} = \frac{1}{2}$ and $\frac{2}{3}$ is more than $\frac{1}{2}$

About the Mathematics in This Unit

Benchmark/Goal	Examples
4. Identify equivalent fractions.	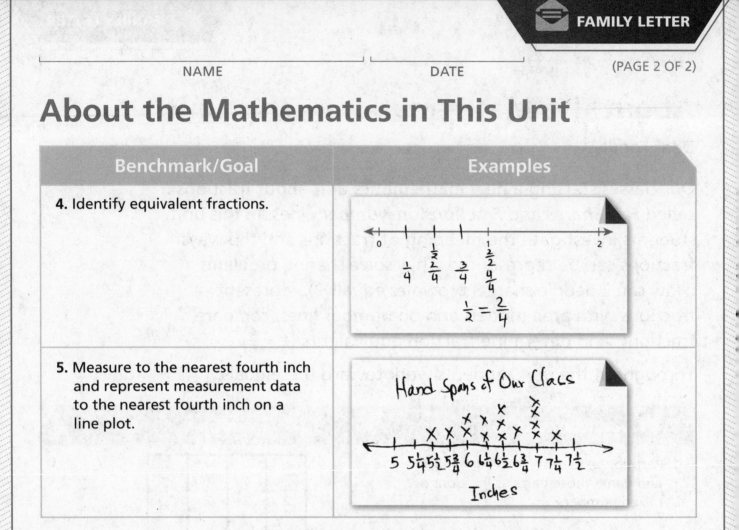
5. Measure to the nearest fourth inch and represent measurement data to the nearest fourth inch on a line plot.	

In our math class, students spend time discussing problems in depth and are asked to share their reasoning and solutions. It is important that children solve math problems in ways that make sense to them. At home, encourage your child to explain the math thinking that supports those solutions.

Please look for more information and activities about *Fair Shares and Fractions on Number Lines* that will be sent home in the coming weeks.

Things That Come in Groups

Solve the story problems below. Write a multiplication equation for each problem and show how you solved it.

A package of juice bars has 6 juice bars.

1 How many juice bars are in 2 packages? _____

Sample Equation: _____ $2 \times 6 = ?$ _____

2 How many juice bars are in 4 packages? _____

Equation: _____

3 How many juice bars are in 8 packages? _____

Equation: _____

NOTE

Students practice multiplication by solving story problems.
MWI Related Multiplication Problems

NAME   DATE

Unit Fractions

Divide each rectangle into the number of pieces indicated. Try to make them as equal as possible, but they do not have to be exactly equal.

 Divide into 4 equal pieces. Color in 1 piece.

What fraction of the rectangle is colored in?

2 Divide into 8 equal pieces. Color in 1 piece.

What fraction of the rectangle is colored in?

3 Divide into 3 equal pieces. Color in 1 piece.

What fraction of the rectangle is colored in?

4 Divide into 6 equal pieces. Color in 1 piece.

What fraction of the rectangle is colored in?

NOTE

Students divide rectangles into fractional pieces and name the fraction pieces.
MWI What Is a Fraction?

Related Activities to Try at Home

Dear Family,

The activities below are related to the mathematics in the fractions unit *Fair Shares and Fractions on Number Lines*. You can use the activities to enrich your child's mathematical learning experience.

Fractions Every Day Take advantage of any natural opportunities to use fractions as they arise. You and your child can share and compare strategies for solving problems such as these:

○ If you cut a whole pizza into 6 equal slices and ate 3 of the slices, what fraction of the pizza did you eat?

○ If you want to share 10 cookies among four people, how can you share them equally? How much does each person get?

○ The gas tank in our car holds 12 gallons, but right now it is only one fourth full. How many gallons of gas do we need to buy to fill up the tank?

Making a Whole In class, your child will be figuring out ways to combine fractions to make a whole, such as $\frac{1}{4} + \frac{3}{4} = 1$. You might build on this while cooking. If a recipe calls for one cup (or one-half cup) of an ingredient, pretend that the measuring cup that holds that amount is missing or broken. Ask your child how else you could measure that amount. What other cups might be combined (for example, $\frac{1}{2} + \frac{1}{4} + \frac{1}{4} = 1$, or $\frac{1}{2} + \frac{1}{2} = 1$)? You might check the prediction by pouring those amounts into the one-cup measure to see whether they fill the cup exactly.

Related Activities to Try at Home

Fraction Scavenger Hunt In class, your child has been exploring fractions and fair shares. To build on this work, you and your child might investigate where and when you use fractions in your home or at the grocery store. You might have a Scavenger Hunt to locate fractions on such things as measuring cups, tools, food packages, in newspapers, and so on.

NAME

DATE

Finding Thirds

Draw lines to divide each shape into thirds.
Label each $\frac{1}{3}$ you create.

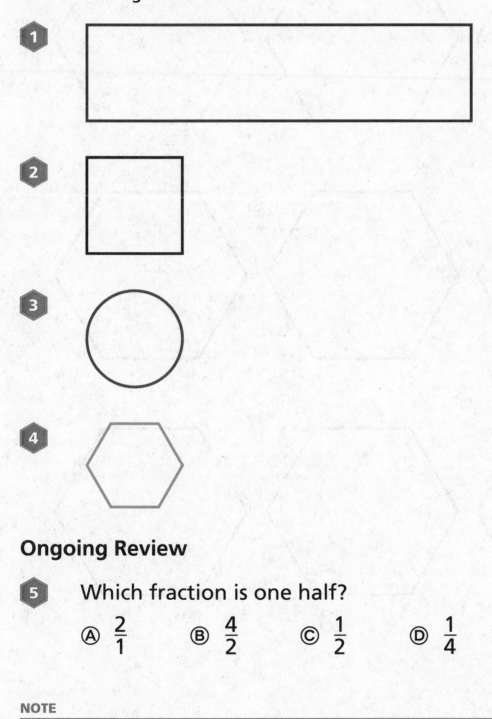

1

2

3

4

Ongoing Review

5 Which fraction is one half?

Ⓐ $\frac{2}{1}$ Ⓑ $\frac{4}{2}$ Ⓒ $\frac{1}{2}$ Ⓓ $\frac{1}{4}$

NOTE

Students are learning that $\frac{1}{3}$ of an area is 1 of 3 equal pieces.
MWI **Fractions of an Area**

NAME

DATE

Hexagon Cookies

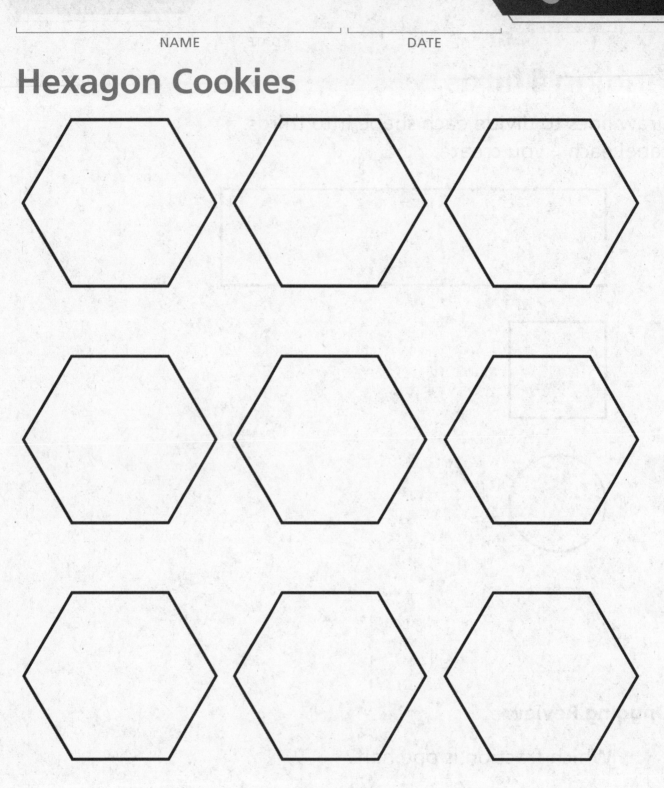

NAME   DATE

Stories About Multiples of 10

For each story problem, solve the problem and show how you solved it.

1 Mr. Bradley has 8 boxes of markers for art projects. Each box contains 50 markers. How many markers does he have in all?

2 Anthony and his friends made 6 bags of peanuts to take to the ballpark. Each bag has 80 peanuts. How many peanuts do they have altogether?

3 Each lap around the school gym is 90 meters. Rachel ran 9 laps. How far did she run?

4 Concert tickets cost 70 dollars each. How much would it cost Nate to get 6 tickets to the concert?

NOTE

Students solve multiplication problems involving multiples of 10.
MWI Multiplying Groups of 10

Fractions on Number Lines

An ant is traveling along the number line. The distance between each of the whole numbers is one block.

1 The ant travels $\frac{1}{2}$ of a block at a time. It rests at each half-block. Mark and label the points where it rests.

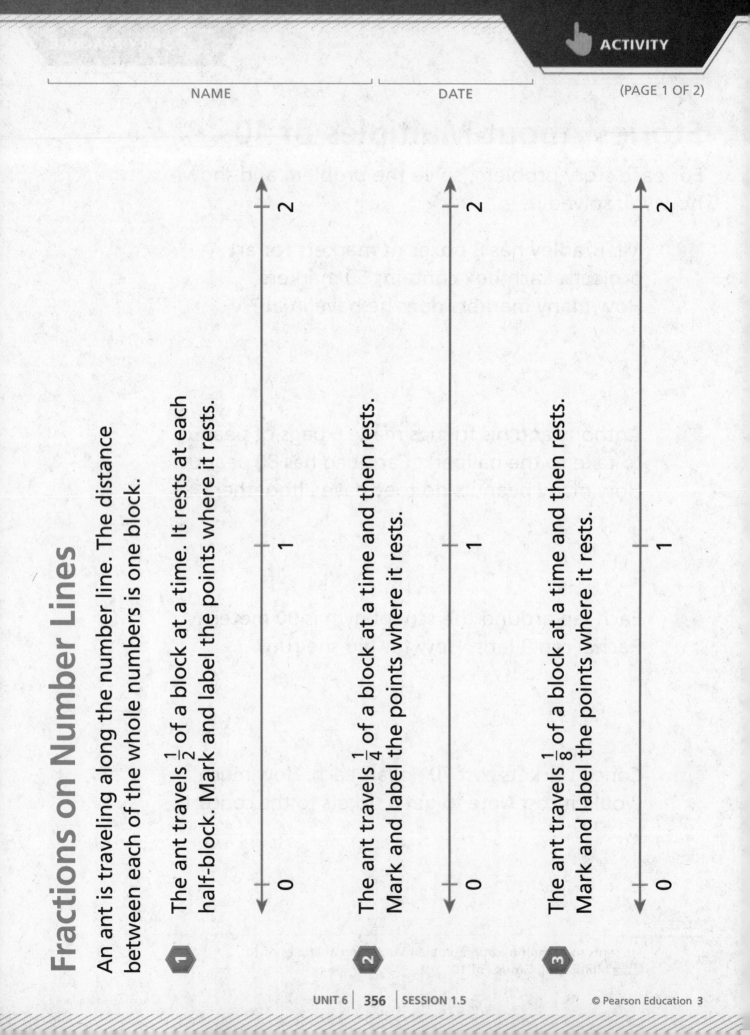

0   1   2

2 The ant travels $\frac{1}{4}$ of a block at a time and then rests. Mark and label the points where it rests.

0   1   2

3 The ant travels $\frac{1}{8}$ of a block at a time and then rests. Mark and label the points where it rests.

0   1   2

Fractions on Number Lines

4 The ant travels $\frac{1}{3}$ of a block at a time and then rests.
Mark and label the points where it rests.

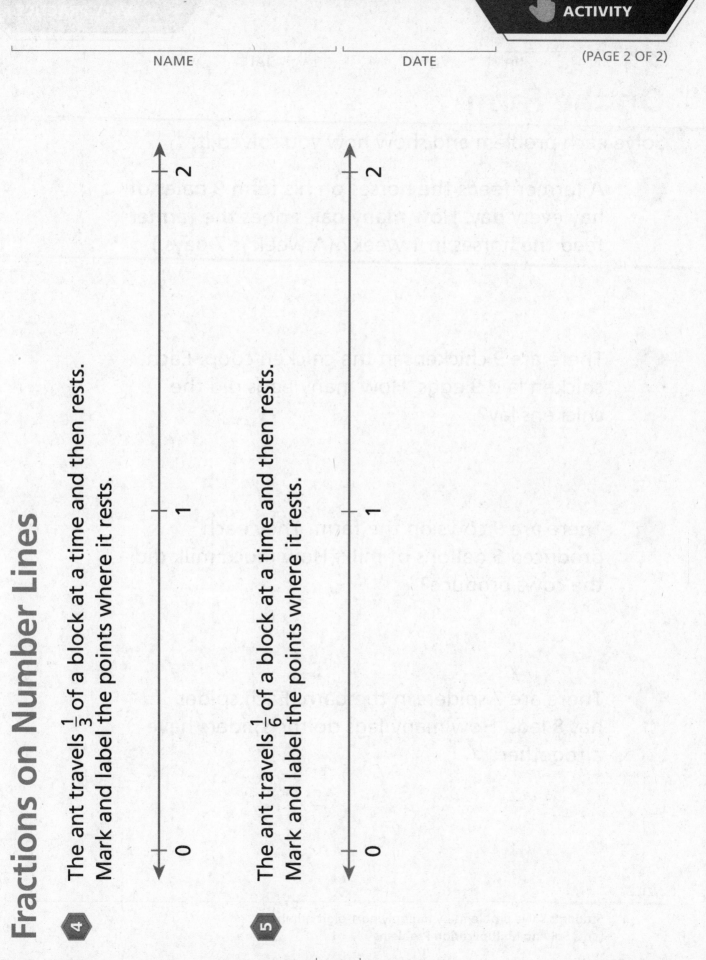

0 — 1 — 2

5 The ant travels $\frac{1}{6}$ of a block at a time and then rests.
Mark and label the points where it rests.

0 — 1 — 2

NAME

DATE

On the Farm

Solve each problem and show how you solved it.

 1 A farmer feeds the horses on his farm 9 bales of hay every day. How many bales does the farmer feed the horses in 1 week? (A week is 7 days.)

 2 There are 9 chickens in the chicken coop. Each chicken laid 9 eggs. How many eggs did the chickens lay?

 3 There are 9 cows on the farm. They each produced 6 gallons of milk. How much milk did the cows produce?

 4 There are 7 spiders in the barn. Each spider has 8 legs. How many legs do the spiders have altogether?

NOTE

Students solve problems by multiplying 1-digit numbers.
MWI **Solving Multiplication Problems**

© Pearson Education 3

NAME _____ DATE _____

Hand Span Data Line Plot

Make a line plot of your class' hand span data.

---

1 What is the shortest hand span in the class? _____

2 What is the longest hand span in the class? _____

3 How many people's hand spans were measured? _____

4 What else do you notice about the data?

NAME _____ DATE _____

Fish Lengths Line Plot

Create a line plot of the following data.

Fourth of July Fishing Competition: Fish Lengths (inches)							
$10\frac{3}{4}$	$15\frac{1}{4}$	$9\frac{1}{2}$	$9\frac{1}{2}$	$11\frac{1}{4}$	14	$10\frac{1}{2}$	$13\frac{3}{4}$
$10\frac{1}{2}$	10	$15\frac{1}{2}$	14	$13\frac{3}{4}$	$9\frac{1}{2}$	$12\frac{1}{4}$	

1 What is the shortest fish length? _____

2 What is the longest fish length? _____

3 What else do you notice about the data?

NOTE

Students make a line plot of measurement data to the nearest $\frac{1}{4}$ inch.

MW1 **Organizing and Representing Data**

© Pearson Education 3

Sharing Several Brownies

_____ brownies shared by _____ people

Draw a picture to show your solution or explain in words how you solved the problem.

How many brownies does each person get? _____

Division Story Problems

Solve each problem and show how you solved it.

1 Sandra wants to plant 49 flowers in 7 equal rows in her garden. How many flowers should she plant in each row?

2 There are 72 players signed up for a basketball league. Each team gets 9 players. How many teams are there?

3 Ashley is sorting muffins equally into 8 boxes for a bake sale. She has 32 muffins. How many should she put in each box?

4 Endris read 60 pages of a book and completed 6 chapters. Each chapter has the same number of pages. How many pages are in each chapter?

NOTE

Students practice solving division problems.

MWI **Solving Division Problems**

NAME   DATE

Are These Equal?

Answer each question. Show your work.

1 Does $\frac{1}{2} = \frac{2}{4}$? _____

Show how you know:

2 Does $\frac{1}{2} + \frac{1}{2} = \frac{2}{4} + \frac{2}{4}$? _____

Show how you know:

3 Does $\frac{2}{8} = \frac{1}{4}$? _____

Show how you know:

NOTE

Students use drawings or stories to show whether these fractions are equivalent.
MWI Equivalent Fractions

NAME

DATE

Identifying and Naming Fractions

Name the fraction that is shaded.

1

2

_____

_____

3

4

_____

_____

Ongoing Review

5 Is this equation true or false? $\frac{1}{4} + \frac{1}{2} = 1$

☐ true ☐ false

NOTE

Students identify and name fractions of rectangles.
MWI **Fractional Parts**

NAME

DATE

How Many Legs?

Solve each story problem. Show how you solved it.

Birds have 2 legs.
Dogs have 4 legs.
Ladybugs have 6 legs.

 There are 48 legs, and they all belong to dogs.
How many dogs are there?

 There are 48 legs, and they all belong to ladybugs.
How many ladybugs are there?

 There are 3 ladybugs, 7 dogs, and 11 birds in the
house. How many legs are there altogether?

NOTE

Students solve multiplication and division problems in story problem contexts.
MWI Solving Division Problems

© Pearson Education 3

NAME

DATE

Least to Greatest

For each set of rectangles below, label the shaded part as a fraction of the rectangle. Then write the fractions in order from least to greatest.

Set 1

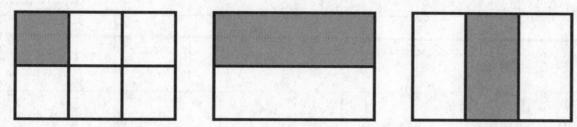

From least to greatest: _____ _____ _____

Set 2

From least to greatest: _____ _____ _____

Choose one of the sets above and tell how you figured out the order from least to greatest.

NOTE

Students practice putting fractions in order from least to greatest.
MWI **Comparing Fractions with the Same Numerator or Denominator**

Comparing Fractions on a Number Line

Use the number lines to solve the problems. Record your solution by using <, >, or =.

1 Ant C walked $\frac{2}{6}$ of the distance from 0 to 1 on the number line, and Ant D walked $\frac{2}{3}$ of the distance from 0 to 1. Who walked farther? Or did the ants walk the same distance? How do you know?

```
←—+————————————————+————————————————+—→
   0                1                2
```

2 Compare $\frac{3}{4}$ and $\frac{6}{8}$ on the number line. Which fraction is greater? Or are the fractions equal? How do you know?

```
←—+————————————————+————————————————+—→
   0                1                2
```

© Pearson Education 3

Comparing Fractions on a Number Line

3   Ant D walked $\frac{4}{8}$ of the distance from 0 to 1 on the number line, and Ant E walked $\frac{5}{8}$ of the distance from 0 to 1. Who walked farther? Or did they walk the same distance? How do you know?

```
0                           1                           2
```

4   Compare $\frac{7}{6}$ and $\frac{7}{3}$ on the number line. Which fraction is greater? Or are the fractions equal? How do you know?

```
0                           1                           2
```

5   Ant F walked $\frac{1}{4}$ of the distance from 0 to 1, and Ant G walked $\frac{2}{8}$ of the distance from 0 to 1. Who walked farther? Or did they walk the same distance? How do you know?

```
0                           1                           2
```

NAME   DATE

Smaller or Equal?

Use the number lines to solve the problems.
Record your solution by using <, >, or =.

1 Compare $\frac{3}{2}$ and $\frac{3}{4}$. Which fraction is smaller?
Or are they equal? How do you know?

```
←—+————————————————+————————————————+—→
   0                1                2
```

2 Compare $\frac{5}{6}$ and $\frac{10}{6}$. Which fraction is smaller?
Or are they equal? How do you know?

```
←—+————————————————+————————————————+—→
   0                1                2
```

3 Ant B walked $\frac{4}{8}$ of the distance from 0 to 1
on the number line, and Ant C walked $\frac{1}{2}$ of the
distance from 0 to 1. Who walked farther?
Or did they walk the same distance?
How do you know?

```
←—+————————————————+————————————————+—→
   0                1                2
```

NOTE

Students place fractions on a number line and compare them.
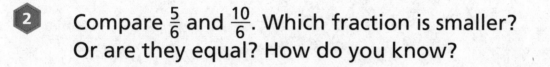 **Fractions on a Number Line**

NAME

DATE

Triangle Paper

More Comparing Fractions

Compare the fractions in each problem. Use brownies, number lines, Fraction Sets, or pattern blocks to show how you know. Record your solution by using $<$, $>$, or $=$ to compare the fractions.

1   Gina ate $\frac{5}{8}$ of a brownie. Chris ate $\frac{5}{6}$ of a brownie. Who ate more? Or did they eat the same amount? Show how you know.

2   Compare $\frac{2}{3}$ and $\frac{4}{6}$. Which fraction is greater? Or are the fractions equal? Show how you know.

3   Gil drank $\frac{2}{6}$ of a glass of milk. Jane drank $\frac{5}{6}$ of a glass of milk. Who drank more? Or did they drink the same amount? Show how you know.

4   On Monday, Keisha ran $\frac{3}{4}$ of a mile, and Becky ran $\frac{3}{6}$ of a mile. Who ran farther? Or did they run the same distance? Show how you know.

More Comparing Fractions

 5 Compare $\frac{7}{8}$ and $\frac{16}{8}$. Which fraction is greater?
Or are the fractions equal? Show how you know.

 6 Compare $\frac{4}{3}$ and $\frac{4}{6}$. Which fraction is greater?
Or are the fractions equal? Show how you know.

 7 Compare $\frac{10}{8}$ and $\frac{5}{4}$. Which fraction is greater?
Or are the fractions equal? Show how you know.

NAME

DATE

Feeding Animals

Solve the following story problems and be sure to show your work.

 At one stable, horses are fed carrot sticks each morning. Each horse eats 6 carrot sticks. How many carrot sticks will 4 horses eat?

 Horses also like to eat apple slices as treats. The stable keeper has 48 apple slices for 4 horses. How many apple slices will each horse get if they are shared equally?

 Fuzzy is the pet rabbit in Ms. Tham's classroom. Fuzzy eats 3 lettuce leaves each day.

a. How many leaves will Fuzzy eat in 6 days?

b. How many leaves will Fuzzy eat in 9 days?

NOTE

Students practice solving multiplication and division problems in story problem contexts.
MWI Solving Multiplication Problems

UNIT 6 | **375** | SESSION 2.3   © Pearson Education 3

NAME

DATE

Comparing Fractions

Compare each pair of fractions. Use words, number lines, or drawings to show how you know. Record your solution by using <, >, or =.

 1 Lily ran $\frac{2}{3}$ of a mile. Sara ran $\frac{1}{3}$ of a mile. Who ran farther? Or did they run the same distance?

Explain or show how you know.

 2 Compare $\frac{5}{6}$ and $\frac{5}{8}$. Which fraction is greater? Or are the fractions equal?

Explain or show how you know.

 3 What is a fraction that is equivalent to $\frac{4}{8}$?

NOTE

Students compare fractions and show how they know which fraction is greater.
MWI **Comparing Fractions with the Same Numerator or Denominator**

NAME

DATE

Multiplication and Division Practice

Solve each multiplication or division problem.

1 $6 \times 90 = $ _____

2 $7 \times 30 = $ _____

3 $5 \times 70 = $ _____

4 $8 \times 50 = $ _____

5 $9 \times 80 = $ _____

6 $80 \times 7 = $ _____

7 $42 \div $ _____ $= 6$

8 $63 \div 7 = $ _____

9 $36 \div 6 = $ _____

10 $32 \div $ _____ $= 4$

NOTE

Students practice solving multiplication and division equations.
MWI **Multiplying Groups of 10**

Counting Around the Class

Answer each question.

1 Ms. Jorge's class counted by 3s. The first person said 3, the second said 6, and the third said 9. How many people counted to get to 36?

How do you know?

2 Mr. Snell's class counted by 8s. The first person said 8, the second said 16, and the third said 24.

a. What number did the 6th person say?

How do you know?

b. What number did the 12th person say?

How do you know?

3 Ms. O'Leary's class counted by 10s. The first person said 10, the second said 20, and the third said 30. There are 24 students in Ms. O'Leary's class. What number did the last person say?

How do you know?

NOTE

Students find the multiples of a given number and solve multiplication problems.
MWI Skip Counting

How Many Miles?

How Many Miles?

NAME   DATE

How Many Liters?

Estimate how many liters you think each container holds. Then measure how many whole liters the container holds.

Container	Estimate	Measurement

NAME _____ DATE _____

Units for Measuring Liquid Volume

Write whether you would use liters or milliliters to measure the liquid volume of each object.

Remember: 1,000 milliliters = 1 liter

1 Fish tank

_____

2 Juice box

_____

Circle the measurement that is more likely.

3 Drinking glass   250 milliliters or 250 liters

4 Bathtub   115 milliliters or 115 liters

5 Pot of soup   6 milliliters or 6 liters

6 Teaspoon   5 milliliters or 5 liters

NAME   DATE

Story Problems About Liquid Volume

Solve each problem. Show your work. Be sure to
include the units in your answer.

 1 A juice carton has 300 milliliters of juice in it.
A different juice carton has 145 milliliters in it.
How much juice is in both cartons?

 2 One morning, a gas station sold 600 liters of
regular gas and 370 liters of super gas. How
much gas did the gas station sell that morning?

 3 Dwayne drank 200 milliliters of milk. Then he
poured 150 milliliters of milk onto his cereal.
How much milk did Dwayne use?

4 A water tank had 180 liters of water in it. When
it rained, the tank filled up with 25 more liters
of water. How much water is in the tank now?

NAME

DATE

Liquid Volume

Write whether you would use liters or milliliters to measure the liquid volume of each object.

1 Ladle

_____

2 Pail

_____

3 Washer

_____

Circle the measurement that is more likely.

4 Milk jug   4 milliliters or 4 liters

5 Eye dropper   5 milliliters or 5 liters

6 Wading pool   120 milliliters or 120 liters

NOTE

Students choose appropriate units of liquid volume.
MWI **Measuring Liquid Volume**

About the Mathematics in This Unit

Dear Family,

Our class is starting a new mathematics unit about addition and subtraction called *How Many Miles?* During this unit, students build on the work from Unit 3 as they practice and refine addition and subtraction strategies working with 3-digit numbers.

Throughout the unit, students work toward these goals:

Benchmark/Goal	Examples
Solve addition and subtraction problems involving masses or volumes.	A juice carton has 300 milliliters of juice in it. A different juice carton has 145 milliliters in it. How much juice is in both cartons?
Solve 3-digit addition problems using at least one strategy fluently.	Solve: $438 + 257$ $\begin{array}{r} 438 \\ +\ 257 \\ \hline 600 \\ 80 \\ +\ 15 \\ \hline 695 \end{array}$ $\begin{array}{r} 438 \\ +\ 200 \\ \hline 638 \\ +\ 50 \\ \hline 688 \\ +\ 7 \\ \hline 695 \end{array}$
Solve 3-digit subtraction problems fluently.	Solve: $\begin{array}{r} 539 \\ -381 \end{array}$ $381 + \underline{19} = 400$ $400 + \underline{139} = 539$ $139 + 19 = 158$ 19 139 381 400 539

© Pearson Education **3**

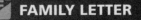
About the Mathematics in This Unit

Benchmark/Goal	Examples
Estimate and measure liquid volume and mass using standard units.	How many liters does the container hold? 

In our math class students spend time discussing problems in depth and are asked to share their reasoning and solutions.

It is important that children accurately and efficiently solve math problems in ways that make sense to them. At home, encourage your child to explain his or her math thinking to you.

Please look for more information and activities related to Unit 7 that will be sent home in the coming weeks.

Units for Measuring Mass

Write whether you would use grams or kilograms to measure the mass of each object.

Remember: 1,000 grams = 1 kilogram

1 Couch

_____

2 Hummingbird

_____

Circle the measurement that is more likely.

3 Glasses   60 grams or 6 kilograms

4 Watermelon   800 grams or 8 kilograms

5 Bag of oranges   20 grams or 2 kilograms

6 Apple   180 grams or 18 kilograms

How Many Grams?

Estimate the mass of each object. Then measure the mass of each.

Object	Estimate	Measurement

Story Problems About Mass

Solve each problem. Show your work. Be sure to include the units in your answer.

1 Chiang used 250 grams of flour to make waffles. Later, she used 130 grams of flour to make muffins. How much flour did she use?

2 An elephant at the zoo ate 92 kilograms of food on Monday, and 119 kilograms of food on Tuesday. How many kilograms of food did the elephant eat in all?

3 Murphy had 500 grams of peanuts. He received 150 more grams of peanuts. What is the mass of the peanuts he has now?

4 A grocer has 75 kilograms of onions, and 115 kilograms of potatoes. What is the total mass of these vegetables?

NAME

DATE

Mass

Write whether you would use grams or kilograms to measure the mass of each object.

1 Safety pin

_____

2 Motorcycle

_____

3 Orange

_____

Circle the measurement that is more likely.

4 Tennis ball   55 grams or 55 kilograms

5 Cat   5 kilograms or 50 kilograms

6 Bunch of grapes   1 gram or 1 kilogram

NOTE

Students choose appropriate measurement units.
MWI **Measuring Mass**

NAME   DATE

More Story Problems

Write an equation. Solve the problem. Show your work.

1   **a.** Kim is packing cookies into bags. She packs
        8 cookies into each of 8 bags. How many
        cookies does she pack?

        b. What if Kim wanted to fill 9 bags with 9 cookies
        each? How many cookies would she need?

2   Mr. Reid's class was counting around the class by
        30s. What number did the 7th person say?

3   The next day, Mr. Reid's class counted around the
        class by 60s. What number did the 7th person say?

NOTE

Students solve multiplication story problems.
MWI Solving Multiplication Problems

© Pearson Education 3

NAME

DATE

100 Grids

Paper Clip Problems

Solve these problems. Show your solutions.
Remember, each box contains 100 paper clips.

 Mrs. Lopez had 3 boxes of paper clips. How
many paper clips did she have? She gave 20 clips
to another teacher. How many clips does she
have left?

 a. Joel and his cousin bought 4 boxes of paper
clips. How many paper clips did they have?

b. They used 45 paper clips for a school project.
How many paper clips do they have now?

Paper Clip Problems

3 Toni and her sister had 500 paper clips. They found 15 more in their mom's desk. They used 65 clips to make a chain. How many paper clips did they have left?

4 **a.** There were 200 paper clips on the shelf in Mr. Vega's classroom. He bought 5 more boxes and put them on the shelf. How many clips were on the shelf then?

b. Later, Mr. Vega took 28 clips. How many paper clips are left on the shelf?

Paper Clip Problems

5   **a.** There were 11 boxes of paper clips in the
third-grade closet. The students from Ms. River's
class used 53 clips. The students from
Ms. Washington's class used one whole box.
How many paper clips were left in the closet?

   b. Later, the students in Mr. Chang's class used
47 paper clips. How many clips are in the
closet now? How many boxes are left?

6   **a.** Heather's mother is an artist. She bought
800 paper clips and used 39 clips to make a wire
sculpture. How many paper clips were left?

   b. Later, Heather's mother used 71 more clips for
her sculpture. Now how many clips are left?

Identifying and Naming Fractions 1

Name the fraction or a mixed number for the shaded part.

1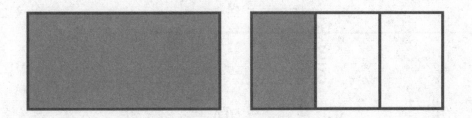

2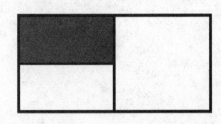

3

Identifying and Naming Fractions 1

Shade in the fraction on the rectangle.

4 $\frac{3}{6}$

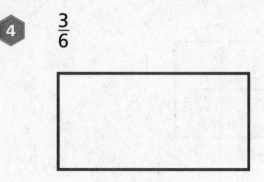

Ongoing Review

Use the number line to solve.

5   Which of the following fractions is equivalent to $\frac{4}{6}$?

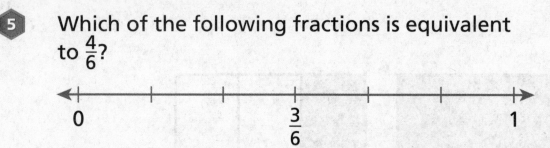

Ⓐ $\frac{2}{6}$ Ⓑ $\frac{1}{2}$ Ⓒ $\frac{4}{8}$ Ⓓ $\frac{2}{3}$

Related Activities to Try at Home

Dear Family,

The activities described here are related to the mathematics in the addition and subtraction unit *How Many Miles?* You can use the activities to enrich your child's mathematical learning experience.

Estimating and Making Change Look for opportunities to practice adding and subtracting with your child in stores and in restaurants.

When you and your child are buying something, figure out together what the change will be. For example, if you buy an item that costs $3.89 and give the clerk $5.00, figure out how much you should get back.

When you buy several things, ask your child to help you estimate how much all the items will cost. For example, if you buy three items that cost $4.95, $3.21, and $7.15, you might ask, "About how many dollars will these items cost?"

People do these problems in many different ways. Whenever these problems come up, encourage your child to figure out ways of estimating and making change, and share your ways of doing it.

Related Activities to Try at Home

Making Sense of Large Numbers With your child, look for large numbers in the newspaper, on packages, on signs, and around your home and neighborhood. Talk about the numbers. For example: *"How much would this television cost if you get a $200 discount?"*

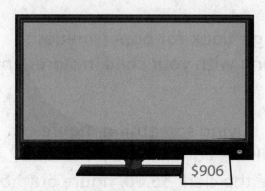

$906

How Did You Solve That? Ask your child to tell you about how he or she is adding and subtracting. Show that you are interested in these approaches. Because these strategies may be unfamiliar to you, listen carefully to your child's explanation; you might even try using the new procedure to do a problem or two yourself. Let your child be the teacher! By explaining their thinking, students increase their understanding of addition and subtraction.

Word Problems About Mass

Solve each problem. Show your work. Be sure to include the units of measure in your answer.

1 Chiang had 400 grams of flour. She used 185 grams of flour to make muffins. How much flour does she have left?

2 The zoo had 200 kilograms of food to feed the reptiles. On Monday, they used 48 kilograms. How much food do they have left?

3 Murphy had 500 grams of peanuts. He ate 225 grams of them. How much does he have left?

4 A young elephant has a mass of 300 kilograms. A young tiger has a mass of 78 kilograms. How much greater is the mass of the elephant?

5 The zoo had 800 kilograms of food to feed their big cats. On Wednesday, they used 202 kilograms. How much food do they have left?

More Comparing Fractions

1 Fill in the missing fractions on the number line.

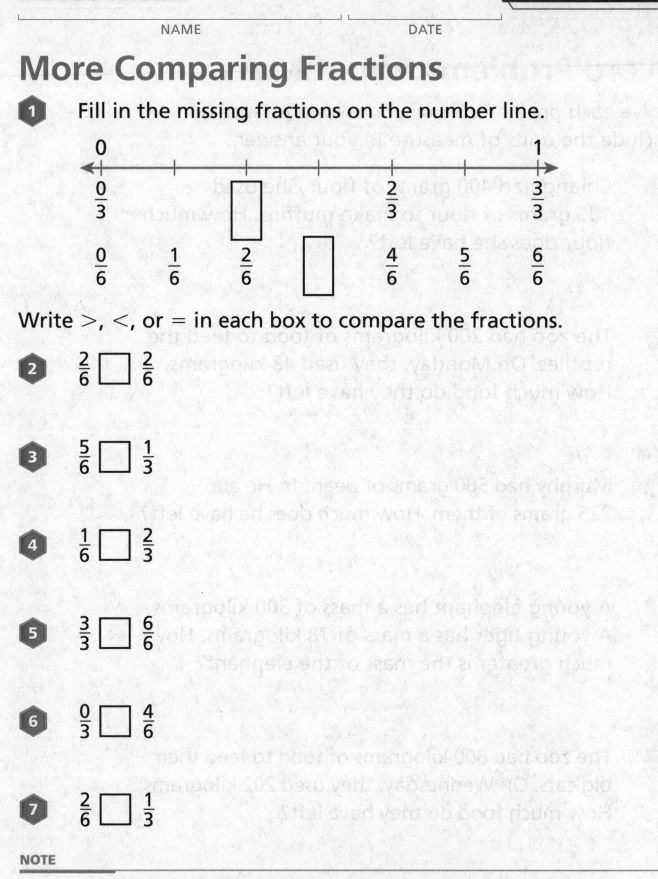

Write >, <, or = in each box to compare the fractions.

2 $\dfrac{2}{6}$ ☐ $\dfrac{2}{6}$

3 $\dfrac{5}{6}$ ☐ $\dfrac{1}{3}$

4 $\dfrac{1}{6}$ ☐ $\dfrac{2}{3}$

5 $\dfrac{3}{3}$ ☐ $\dfrac{6}{6}$

6 $\dfrac{0}{3}$ ☐ $\dfrac{4}{6}$

7 $\dfrac{2}{6}$ ☐ $\dfrac{1}{3}$

NOTE

Students label fractions on a number line and compare fractions.
MWI **Fractions on a Number Line**

NAME   DATE

Boxes of Crayons

Solve these problems. Show your solutions.
Each box of crayons contains 100 crayons.

 a. The art teacher had 400 crayons in his classroom. He bought 3 more boxes. How many crayons does he have?

b. At the end of the day, 34 crayons were broken. How many whole crayons does the art teacher have left?

 Emily and Marshall each have 2 boxes of crayons. Emily gave 58 crayons to her younger sister.

a. How many crayons does Emily have left?

b. How many crayons does Marshall have?

c. How many crayons do they have all together?

NOTE

Students solve problems that involve combining and then subtracting from groups of 100.
MWI **Subtraction Strategies: Adding Up and Subtracting Back**

NAME   DATE

Related Subtraction Problems

As you work on these problems, think about how they are related and how some of the problems help you solve others.

Set 1	**Set 2**
100 − 90 = _____	100 − 93 = _____
300 − 90 = _____	300 − 93 = _____
330 − 90 = _____	500 − 93 = _____
430 − 90 = _____	520 − 93 = _____

Set 3

$$200 \quad 300 \quad 500 \quad 500$$
$$-150 \quad -150 \quad -150 \quad -250$$

Set 4

100 − 85 = _____
115 − 85 = _____
215 − 85 = _____
215 − 185 = _____

Set 5

$$300 \quad 300 \quad 500 \quad 540$$
$$-75 \quad -175 \quad -175 \quad -175$$

Set 6

200 − 60 = _____
300 − 60 = _____
200 − 55 = _____
300 − 55 = _____

Choose one problem set. On another sheet of paper, explain how you used each problem in the set to solve the next problem.

Word Problems About Liquid Volume

Solve each problem. Show your work. Be sure to include the units of measure in your answer.

1 A milk carton had 500 milliliters of milk in it. Phillip poured 89 milliliters into a glass. How much milk is left in the carton?

2 A water tank had 300 liters of water in it. Kim used 45 liters to water the garden. How much water is still in the tank?

3 An aquarium had 200 liters of water in it. A small crack appeared, and 37 liters leaked out before it was fixed. How much water is still in the aquarium?

4 A water bottle held 800 milliliters of water. Kate drank 94 milliliters. How much water is still in the bottle?

5 A gas tank on a big truck has 100 liters of gas in it. If 84 liters of gas are used, how much will be left in the tank?

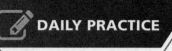
NAME

DATE

Identifying and Naming Fractions 2

Name the fraction or a mixed number for the shaded part.

1

_____

2

_____

Draw a number line. Then locate and label the fraction shown.

3 $\frac{2}{3}$

4 $\frac{2}{2}$

Ongoing Review

5 Which of the following fractions names point K on the number line? Mark the correct answer.

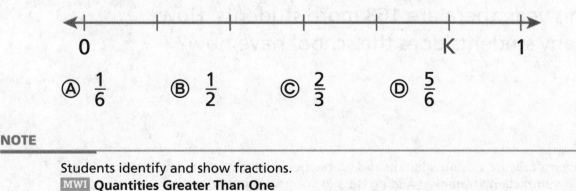

(A) $\frac{1}{6}$ (B) $\frac{1}{2}$ (C) $\frac{2}{3}$ (D) $\frac{5}{6}$

NOTE

Students identify and show fractions.
MWI Quantities Greater Than One

How Many Students?

For each problem, write an equation, solve the problem, and show your solution.

 1 South City School has 427 girls and 353 boys. How many students does the school have altogether?

 2 Riverside School had 517 students last year. This year, 60 students moved away before school started. How many students does the school have now?

 3 Westburg School has 284 students altogether. There are 136 girls. How many boys are there in the school?

 4 Ocean View School had 641 students last year. This year, there are 168 more students. How many students does the school have now?

NOTE

Students practice solving addition and subtraction problems in story contexts.
MWI **Subtraction Strategies: Adding Up and Subtracting Back**

NAME   DATE

More Related Subtraction Problems

Solve the first problem in each set and show your solution. Then solve the next two problems to see how some problems help you solve others.

Set 1	Set 2
First solve: 93 − 67 = _____	First solve: 84 − 28 = _____
Now solve these: 193 − 67 = _____ 293 − 67 = _____	Now solve these: 184 − 28 = _____ 384 − 28 = _____

Set 3	Set 4

First solve: 126
         − 65
	First solve: 130
	         − 75

Now solve these:
 	
  226   226
  − 65   − 165
	Now solve these:
	
	  330 330
	  − 75 − 175

More Paper Clip Problems

Solve these problems. Show your solutions. Remember, each box contains 100 paper clips.

 1 There were 6 boxes of paper clips in the office of Springdale School. On Monday, the secretary used 62 paper clips. How many clips were left?

 2 Ms. Valentine had 900 paper clips. Her students used 262 clips to make a display for Family Math Night. How many paper clips were left?

 3 **a.** There were 15 boxes of paper clips in the Rosewood Company supply room. On Monday, someone took 35 paper clips from one box. How many paper clips were left in the supply room?

b. On Tuesday, someone took 25 more clips from that box. How many paper clips were in the supply room then?

_____   _____
        NAME   DATE

Making Estimates

First, estimate the answer to each problem. Then, solve the problem and show your solution. Each full crayon box contains 100 crayons.

1 Jay had 4 boxes of crayons. He gave 67 crayons to Erika. How many crayons does he have left?

Estimate: _____

Solution:

2 Rachel had 173 crayons. Her mother gives her a new box, and she finds 18 more crayons in her desk drawer. How many crayons does Rachel have now?

Estimate: _____

Solution:

3 There were 517 crayons in a bucket. Laura took 69 crayons home. How many crayons are left in the bucket?

Estimate: _____

Solution:

Ongoing Review

  What is the greatest number of dimes you need to make $4.72?

Ⓐ 7 　　　　 Ⓑ 40 　　　　 Ⓒ 47 　　　　 Ⓓ 72

NOTE
_____

Students first estimate and then solve addition and subtraction problems.
MWI **Adding and Subtracting Tens and Hundreds**

NAME

DATE

More Story Problems About Liquid Volume

Solve each problem. Show your work. Be sure to include the units in your answer.

1 Gina drank 300 milliliters of orange juice. Then she drank 235 milliliters of grape juice. How much juice did Gina drink in all?

2 At the start of a class field trip, a bus had 122 liters of gasoline in the tank. When it returned to school, the bus had used 48 liters of gasoline. How many liters of gas were left in the tank?

3 A pool can hold 520 liters of water. If the pool is filled with 300 liters of water, how much more water can the pool hold?

4 An elephant drank 153 liters of water on Monday and 219 liters of water on Tuesday. How many liters of water did the elephant drink in all?

NOTE

Students solve problems about liquid volume.
MWI Measuring Liquid Volume

NAME _____   DATE _____

Subtraction Practice

Solve these problems. Show your solutions. You may draw a number line to help explain your thinking.

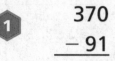
1
$$\begin{array}{r} 370 \\ -\ 91 \\ \hline \end{array}$$

2   277 − 62 = _____

3   456 − 228 = _____

4   346 − 297 = _____

NOTE

Students practice solving subtraction problems with 2- and 3-digit numbers.
MWI Subtraction Strategies: Subtracting One Number in Parts

Practice with Related Subtraction Problems 1

As you work, think about how the problems in each set are related and how some of the problems help you solve others.

Set 1	Set 2
100 − 35 = _____	100 − 67 = _____
200 − 35 = _____	300 − 67 = _____
380 − 35 = _____	600 − 67 = _____
380 − 135 = _____	640 − 67 = _____

Set 3

$$\begin{array}{cccc} 500 & 600 & 700 & 750 \\ -\,215 & -\,215 & -\,215 & -\,215 \end{array}$$

Set 4

100 − 95 = _____

300 − 95 = _____

500 − 95 = _____

583 − 95 = _____

Ongoing Review

Solve the problem. Mark the correct answer.

443 − 20 + 100 − 15 = _____

Ⓐ 415　　　Ⓑ 418　　　Ⓒ 508　　　Ⓓ 515

NOTE

Students continue to practice solving related subtraction problems.
MWI Subtraction Strategies: Subtracting One Number in Parts

Addition Starter Problems

In each set, solve all three starter problems. Then solve the final problem. Show your solution. Use one of the starter problems to help you.

Set 1

$100 + 600 =$ _____

$150 + 650 =$ _____

$152 + 600 =$ _____

Final problem: $152 + 683 =$ _____

Show your solution.

Set 2

$400 + 200 =$ _____

$429 + 200 =$ _____

$430 + 200 =$ _____

Final problem: $429 + 266 =$ _____

Show your solution.

Addition Starter Problems

In each set, solve all three starter problems. Then solve the final problem. Show your solution. Use one of the starter problems to help you.

Set 3

30 + 90 = _____

835 + 100 = _____

97 + 3 = _____

Final problem: 835 + 97 = _____

Show your solution.

Set 4

700 + 346 = _____

700 + 300 = _____

709 + 340 = _____

Final problem: 709 + 346 = _____

Show your solution.

Addition Starter Problems

In each set, solve all three starter problems. Then solve the final problem. Show your solution. Use one of the starter problems to help you.

Set 5

$500 + 300 =$ _____

$584 + 300 =$ _____

$378 + 2 =$ _____

Final problem: $584 + 378 =$ _____

Show your solution.

Set 6

$600 + 400 =$ _____

$630 + 470 =$ _____

$488 + 12 =$ _____

Final problem: $636 + 488 =$ _____

Show your solution.

NAME   DATE

More Story Problems About Mass

Solve each problem. Show your work. Be sure to include the units in your answer.

1 A baker has 140 kilograms of flour and 232 kilograms of sugar in her bakery. What is the total mass of these ingredients?

2 An adult orca whale needs 280 kilograms of food each week. If an orca eats 148 kilograms of food by the middle of the week, how much more food will the orca need to eat during the rest of the week?

3 Edwin and Kim are making vegetable soup. They use 168 grams of onions, 134 grams of carrots, 102 grams of celery, and 194 grams of tomatoes. What is the total mass of their soup ingredients?

4 Denzel put 453 grams of birdseed in his bird feeder. Many birds came to the feeder. The birds ate 364 grams of the birdseed. How much birdseed does Denzel have left now?

NOTE

Students solve problems about mass.
MWI **Measuring Mass**

© Pearson Education 3

NAME

DATE

Addition and Subtraction: Related Problems 1

As you work, think about how the problems in each set are related and how some of the problems help you solve others.

Set 1

$250 - 60 =$ _____

$250 - 65 =$ _____

$250 - 67 =$ _____

$255 - 67 =$ _____

Set 2

$130 + 200 =$ _____

$130 + 190 =$ _____

$130 + 180 =$ _____

$132 + 180 =$ _____

Set 3

$$\begin{array}{r} 70 \\ +\ 90 \\ \hline \end{array} \qquad \begin{array}{r} 170 \\ +\ 90 \\ \hline \end{array} \qquad \begin{array}{r} 370 \\ +\ 90 \\ \hline \end{array} \qquad \begin{array}{r} 370 \\ +290 \\ \hline \end{array}$$

Set 4

$420 - 20 =$ _____

$415 - 20 =$ _____

$415 - 120 =$ _____

$415 - 220 =$ _____

NOTE

Students use what they know from solving one problem to help them solve related addition and subtraction problems.

MWI Subtraction Strategies: Subtracting One Number in Parts

© Pearson Education 3

Solving Addition Problems

Solve each problem and show your solution. For each story problem, solve the problem and write an equation to go with it.

 1 $425 + 288 = $ _____

 2
$$
\begin{array}{r}
623 \\
+\ 249 \\
\hline
\end{array}
$$

3   Ms. Shaw had 5 boxes of paper clips in her classroom closet and another 74 clips on her desk. She bought 3 more boxes and found 28 more clips in her desk drawer. Each box contains 100 paper clips. How many paper clips does she have now?

Solving Addition Problems

Solve each problem and show your solution. For each story problem, solve the problem and write an equation to go with it.

4
$$758$$
$$+\ 76$$

5 930 + 377 = _____

6 Hannah and her sister both collect pennies. Hannah has 561 pennies, and her sister has 459 pennies. If they put all their pennies together, how many will they have? How much is that in dollars and cents?

NAME _____ DATE _____

More Addition Starter Problems

In each set, solve all three starter problems. Then solve the final problem. Show your solution. Use one of the starter problems to help you.

Set 1

200 + 500 = _____

233 + 500 = _____

595 + 5 = _____

Final problem: 233 + 595 = _____

Show your solution.

Set 2

200 + 700 = _____

280 + 700 = _____

286 + 700 = _____

Final problem: 286 + 707 = _____

Show your solution.

Ongoing Review

If you have 1,005 bottle caps, how many piles of 100 could you have?
Mark the correct answer.

Ⓐ 100   Ⓑ 10   Ⓒ 5   Ⓓ 1

NOTE

Students solve a variety of possible "first steps" before solving a final addition problem.
MWI Addition Strategies: Changing the Numbers

Adding More Than Two Numbers

For each problem, first estimate about how many hundreds the answer will have. Then solve the problem and show your solution.

1 343 + 487 + 55 = _____

About how many hundreds? _____

Solution:

2 Zhang bought some fruit at the market. The apple had a mass of 145 grams, the mango had a mass of 628 grams, and the kiwi had a mass of 37 grams. What was the total mass of the fruit?

About how many hundreds? _____

Solution:

3 The pet store owner needs to fill three fish tanks with water. One tank has a liquid volume of 245 liters, another 386 liters, and the third one has a liquid volume of 465 liters. How much water does the owner need to fill all three tanks?

About how many hundreds? _____

Solution:

Adding More Than Two Numbers

For each problem, first estimate about how many hundreds the answer will have. Then solve the problem and show your solution.

4 $801 + 27 + 446 =$ _____

About how many hundreds? _____

Solution:

5   The zookeeper received a shipment of food. The fish food had a mass of 78 kilograms, the reptile food had a mass of 296 kilograms, and the primate food had a mass of 813 kilograms. What was the total mass of the food?

6 $190 + 791 + 359 =$ _____

About how many hundreds? _____

Solution:

NAME

DATE

More Addition Problems

Solve each problem and show your solution.

1 $451 + 546 = $ _____	**2** $316 + 490 = $ _____
3 $298 + 548 = $ _____	**4** $135 + 821 = $ _____
5 $276 + 765 = $ _____	**6** $386 + 331 = $ _____
7 $502 + 799 = $ _____	**8** $738 + 834 = $ _____

NAME   DATE

Representing and Comparing Fractions

1 Divide the zero-to-one number line in eighths.
Label each eighth.

0 ←————————————————————————→ 1

Label the following points on the number line above.

2 Point A: $\frac{1}{4}$

3 Point B: $\frac{1}{2}$

4 Point C: $\frac{3}{8}$

5 Point D: $\frac{3}{4}$

Write >, <, or = in each box to compare the fractions.

6 $\frac{1}{4}$ ☐ $\frac{3}{4}$

7 $\frac{4}{8}$ ☐ $\frac{1}{2}$

8 $\frac{3}{8}$ ☐ $\frac{3}{4}$

9 $\frac{8}{8}$ ☐ $\frac{0}{8}$

NOTE

Students label fractions on a number line and compare fractions.
MWI **Fractions on a Number Line**

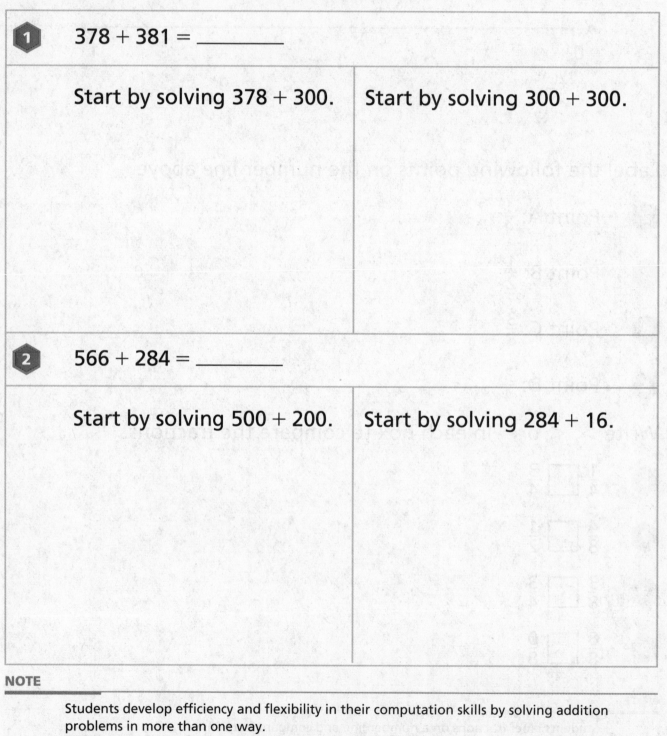
NAME _____ DATE _____

Two Ways to Solve a Problem

Solve each problem in two ways, using each of the
first steps below. Show your solutions.

1 378 + 381 = _____

| Start by solving 378 + 300. | Start by solving 300 + 300. |

2 566 + 284 = _____

| Start by solving 500 + 200. | Start by solving 284 + 16. |

NOTE

Students develop efficiency and flexibility in their computation skills by solving addition
problems in more than one way.

MWI Addition Strategies: Changing the Numbers

© Pearson Education 3

Addition and Subtraction: Related Problems 2

1 Solve each set of related problems.

Set 1	**Set 2**
400 + 200 = _____	500 − 50 = _____
401 + 201 = _____	500 − 60 = _____
399 + 198 = _____	500 − 62 = _____

Set 3

$$
\begin{array}{r} 300 \\ 300 \\ +\,300 \\ \hline \end{array}
\qquad
\begin{array}{r} 298 \\ 297 \\ +\,301 \\ \hline \end{array}
\qquad
\begin{array}{r} 310 \\ 290 \\ +\,295 \\ \hline \end{array}
$$

Set 4

$$
\begin{array}{r} 1{,}000 \\ -\,50 \\ \hline \end{array}
\qquad
\begin{array}{r} 900 \\ -\,50 \\ \hline \end{array}
\qquad
\begin{array}{r} 702 \\ -\,50 \\ \hline \end{array}
$$

2 Pick one problem set. Explain how you used some of the problems in the set to solve others.

NOTE

Students use what they know from solving one problem to help them solve related addition and subtraction problems.

MWI Addition Strategies: Changing the Numbers

The Oregon Trail

Solve these problems about a journey by covered wagon. Use this map to help you. Show your solutions for each problem on a separate piece of paper.

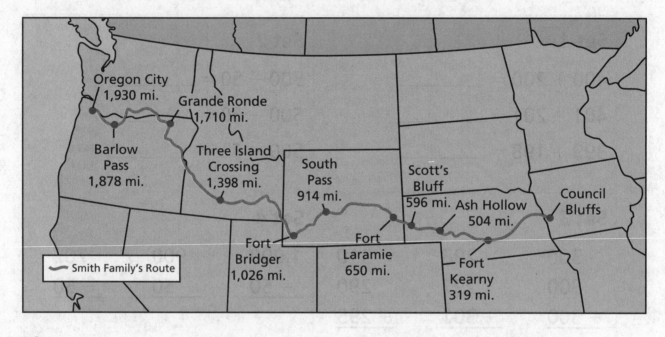

Oregon City 1,930 mi.
Grande Ronde 1,710 mi.
Barlow Pass 1,878 mi.
Three Island Crossing 1,398 mi.
South Pass 914 mi.
Scott's Bluff 596 mi.
Ash Hollow 504 mi.
Council Bluffs
Fort Bridger 1,026 mi.
Fort Laramie 650 mi.
Fort Kearny 319 mi.
Smith Family's Route

1 It's 1847, and the Smith family sets out from Council Bluffs, Iowa. In the first two weeks, they travel 319 miles to Fort Kearny. At the end of the first month, they cross the Platte River at Ash Hollow. They have traveled 504 miles since their trip began. How far did they travel from Fort Kearny to Ash Hollow?

2 After leaving Ash Hollow, the Smiths arrive at Scott's Bluff. They rest for several days. Scott's Bluff is 596 miles from the start of the trail. How far did they travel from Ash Hollow to Scott's Bluff?

The Oregon Trail

3 When the family arrives at Fort Laramie, they are 650 miles from the start of the trail. How far did they travel from Scott's Bluff to Fort Laramie?

4 The Smiths cross the Continental Divide at South Pass, which is 914 miles from the start of the trail. How far is Fort Laramie from South Pass?

5 Fort Bridger is 1,026 miles from the start of the Smiths' trip. When they reach Three Island Crossing, they are 1,398 miles from their start. How far is it from Fort Bridger to Three Island Crossing?

6 Before reaching Barlow Pass, the family rests at Grande Ronde. They are 1,710 miles from the beginning of the trail. How far did they travel from Three Island Crossing to Grande Ronde?

7 At Barlow Pass, the Smiths' horses are tired. They have walked 1,878 miles on this trip! How far is it from Grande Ronde to Barlow Pass?

8 Finally, the Smiths arrive in Oregon City. They have traveled 1,930 miles altogether. How many miles was the last leg of their journey, from Barlow Pass to Oregon City?

NAME _____ DATE _____

Practice with Adding More Than Two Numbers

For each problem, first estimate about how many hundreds the answer will have. Then solve the problem and show your solution.

1 $312 + 588 + 375 = $ _____

About how many hundreds? _____

Solution:

2 $667 + 385 + 298 = $ _____

About how many hundreds? _____

Solution:

3 $79 + 385 + 412 = $ _____

About how many hundreds? _____

Solution:

Ongoing Review

4 Which expression is more than 1,000? Mark the correct answer.

Ⓐ $358 + 512 + 98$ Ⓒ $668 + 55 + 459$

Ⓑ $299 + 510 + 127$ Ⓓ $125 + 225 + 450$

NOTE

Students solve addition problems with more than two addends.
MWI Adding More Than Two Numbers

NAME _____ DATE _____

Addition Starter Problems

Solve each problem two ways, using the first steps listed below. Show your work clearly.

1   157 + 664 = _____

Start by solving 100 + 600.	Start by solving 150 + 650.

2   719 + 384 = _____

Start by solving 700 + 384.	Start by solving 19 + 81.

NOTE

Students practice solving addition problems. They work on efficiency and flexibility by solving the same problem in two different ways.

MWI **Addition Strategies: Changing the Numbers**

Write and Solve a Subtraction Problem 1

1 Write a story problem to go with this problem.

$352 - 168 =$ _____

2 Solve the problem and show your solution.

Our Collections

For each problem, write an equation that represents the problem, solve the problem, and show your solution.

 Deondra collects coins. She had 385 coins in her collection. On her birthday her uncle gave her 125 more coins to add to her collection. How many coins does Deondra have now?

 Oscar collects comic books. He has 462 superhero comic books and 394 cartoon comic books. How many comic books does he have altogether?

NOTE

Students solve addition and subtraction problems in a story problem context.
MWI Subtraction Strategies: Adding Up and Subtracting Back

Our Collections

3 Nancy collects toy cars. She had 429 in her collection. She sold 180 of them to a friend. How many toy cars does Nancy have left?

4 Adam collects flag stickers. He had 534 in his collection. He gave 172 of them away to the history teacher. How many flag stickers does Adam have left?

NAME _____ DATE _____

Addition Practice

Solve each addition problem. Show you work.

 1   447 + 328 = _____

2   251 + 779 = _____

3   388 + 344 = _____

 4   623 + 459 = _____

NOTE

Students practice solving addition problems with 3-digit numbers.

MWI **Addition Strategies: Adding by Place**

How Much Change?

Answer these questions. You may use play money to help you.

 1 At the grocery store, you spend $1.49.

    a. How much change will you get if you pay with two one-dollar bills ($2.00)? _____

    b. How much change will you get if you pay with a five-dollar bill ($5.00)? _____

    c. How much change will you get if you pay with a ten-dollar bill ($10.00)? _____

 2 At the trading card store, you spend $3.78.

    a. How much change will you get if you pay with four one-dollar bills ($4.00)? _____

    b. How much change will you get if you pay with a five-dollar bill ($5.00)? _____

    c. How much change will you get if you pay with a ten-dollar bill ($10.00)? _____

How Much Change?

3 At the snack bar, you spend $4.25.

    a. How much change will you get if you pay with a five-dollar bill ($5.00)?   _____

    b. How much change will you get if you pay with a ten-dollar bill ($10.00)?   _____

    c. How much change will you get if you pay with a twenty-dollar bill ($20.00)?   _____

Earning and Spending

Solve these problems. Show your solutions.

1 Marisa earned $7.75 babysitting for her cousin. She spent $5.98 on a birthday present for her best friend. How much money did she have left?

2 Josh earned $8.10 collecting and returning bottles for recycling. He spent $2.85 at the arcade. How much money did he have left?

3 Zhang earned $6.25 walking the dog for his neighbors. He spent $4.27 on a new comic book. How much money did he have left?

4 Julia earned $9.50 doing chores for her grandfather. She spent $6.90 at the movies. How much money did she have left?

More How Much Change?

Answer the following questions. You may use play money to help you.

 At the grocery store, you spend $1.79.

   a. How much is your change if you pay with two 1-dollar bills ($2.00)? _____

   b. How much is your change if you pay with a 5-dollar bill ($5.00)? _____

   c. How much is your change if you pay with a 10-dollar bill ($10.00)? _____

 At the trading card store, you spend $3.24.

   a. How much is your change if you pay with four 1-dollar bills ($4.00)? _____

   b. How much is your change if you pay with a 5-dollar bill ($5.00)? _____

   c. How much is your change if you pay with a 10-dollar bill ($10.00)? _____

NOTE

Students solve subtraction problems using the context of money.

MWI Subtraction Strategies: Subtracting One Number in Parts

More How Much Change?

3 At the snack bar, you spend $4.48.

   a. How much is your change if you pay
      with a 5-dollar bill ($5.00)? _____

   b. How much is your change if you pay
      with a 10-dollar bill ($10.00)? _____

   c. How much is your change if you pay
      with a 20-dollar bill ($20.00)? _____

Solving Subtraction Problems

Solve each problem. Show your solutions.

1 Some of the students at Riverside School walk to school. All of the other students take the bus. There are 404 students in the school. 166 of them take the bus. How many walk to school?

2 On Monday, 339 children had the school lunch. On Tuesday, 252 children had the school lunch. How many more children had the school lunch on Monday than on Tuesday?

3 The Ortiz family traveled to the Washington Zoo, which is 264 miles away from their home. When they stopped for lunch, they had gone 117 miles. How many more miles did they have to travel after lunch?

4 The Asian History Museum had 324 Japanese stamps. They sold all the samurai stamps to a collector. Now the museum has 291 stamps in its collection. How many stamps did the museum sell?

Solving Subtraction Problems

Solve each problem. Show your solutions.

 5   436 − 219 = _____

6   315 − 288 = _____

 7   527 − 174 = _____

8   764 − 248 = _____

NAME

DATE

Coupon Savings

These coupons are from a newspaper ad.

1 Find and list coupons with savings that add up to $3.00.

2 Find and list three coupons with savings that add up to $1.50.

3 Will the savings on cereal, yogurt, and eggs be more or less than $2.00? Explain.

Ongoing Review

4 Which expression equals 159?

Ⓐ 10 + 58 + 100

Ⓒ 200 − 41

Ⓑ 118 + 30 + 1

Ⓓ 250 − 100 − 50

NOTE

Students find combinations of numbers that equal given amounts.
MWI Adding More Than Two Numbers

NAME   DATE

Problems About Money

Solve these problems. Show your solutions.

 Eve had $4.75 in her piggy bank. She earned
$2.50 babysitting. How much money does Eve
have now?

 $3.28 + $7.46 = _____

 Marcus had $5.98 in his wallet. He bought a
notebook for $2.68. How much money does
Marcus have now?

 $6.00 − $1.49 = _____

NOTE

Students practice solving addition and subtraction problems in the context of money.
MWI Subtraction Strategies: Adding Up and Subtracting Back

Book Orders

Title	Price	Title	Price
Monster Jokes	$1.99	Silly Kid Jokes	$3.42
10 Projects with Wood	$1.73	10 Projects with Paper	$2.54
Mystery of Owl Island	$2.50	Mystery of the Silver Wolf	$3.35
Going West	$4.28	About America	$4.46
Time Machine	$3.15	Upside-Down Town	$4.25

If you have $10.00, which books can you buy? Find combinations of at least three different books that cost close to $10.00 in all. Then find how much money you have left. Write equations to show your solutions.

Book Order 1 List titles and prices.

_____   _____

_____   _____

How much did you spend? _____ How much is left? _____

Equations:

Book Order 2 List titles and prices.

_____   _____

_____   _____

How much did you spend? _____ How much is left? _____

Equations:

Book Orders

Title	Price	Title	Price
Monster Jokes	$1.99	Silly Kid Jokes	$3.42
10 Projects with Wood	$1.73	10 Projects with Paper	$2.54
Mystery of Owl Island	$2.50	Mystery of the Silver Wolf	$3.35
Going West	$4.28	About America	$4.46
Time Machine	$3.15	Upside-Down Town	$4.25

Find other combinations of at least three different books that cost close to $10.00 in all. For one order, find a combination of at least four books.

Book Order 3 List titles and prices.

_____ _____

_____ _____

How much did you spend? _____ How much is left? _____

Equations:

Book Order 4 List titles and prices.

_____ _____

_____ _____

How much did you spend? _____ How much is left? _____

Equations:

Two-Step Money Problems

Solve these problems. Show your solutions.

 1   Lakesha had $4.75 in her piggy bank. She spent
$3.29 on a present for her sister. Then she earned
$2.00 sweeping the front steps for a neighbor.
How much money does Lakesha have now?

 2   Greg had $8.15 in his wallet. He spent $5.87 on
a sandwich. Then his friend paid him back $7.50
that he owed him. How much money does Greg
have now?

Two-Step Money Problems

3 Mike earned $12.20 babysitting. He went to the card store and spent $6.49. Then he went to the science store and spent $4.80. How much money does Mike have now?

4 Cammy had $9.36 that she saved in pennies. She earned $6.40 doing chores for her grandfather. Then she spent $8.68 on a new book. How much money does Cammy have now?

Who Gets More?

1 Today the students in Mr. Wong's room have blueberry muffins to share. Each group gets 8 muffins to share equally.

Group A: 6 students share 8 muffins.

Group B: 5 students share 8 muffins.

Which students get the larger share, Group A or Group B?

Tell how you decided. Use words and drawings to help you explain.

NOTE

Students solve two sharing problems and compare the answers.
MWI **Fractional Parts**

NAME _____ DATE _____

How Many Altogether?

1 How many students altogether go to these three schools?

Elm Street School	Valley School	Oak Park School
567 students	275 students	404 students

About how many hundreds in all? Estimate. _____

How did you decide on your estimate?

_____

_____

Add the numbers to find the exact total. _____

2 How much money will Sophie spend for these school supplies?

Notebook $2.99	Pen $1.79	Markers $3.95

About how many dollars in all? Estimate. _____

How did you decide on your estimate?

_____

_____

Add the numbers to find the exact total. _____

NOTE

Students make estimates and then solve addition problems with more than two addends.
MWI Adding More Than Two Numbers

NAME

DATE

Count Your Change

1 Complete this chart.

Item Bought	Cost of Item	Amount Given to Clerk	Amount of Change
Ruler	$0.47	$1.00	
Sandwich	$3.18	$5.00	
Seeds	$1.55		$0.45
Socks	$2.74		$2.26
Shampoo		$1.00	$0.11
Taffy apple		$5.00	$4.10
Stickers	$1.16	$10.00	
Magazine		$10.00	$6.35

Ongoing Review

2 How much greater is 147 than 85?

Ⓐ 43   Ⓑ 51   Ⓒ 53   Ⓓ 62

NOTE

Students solve subtraction problems in the context of money.
MWI Subtractions Strategies: Subtracting One Number in Parts

Plan a Meal

Doctors say you should eat meat or beans, grains, fruits, and vegetables every day. It is suggested that a third grader eat between 600 and 800 calories for dinner.

Food	Calories	Food	Calories
Peanut butter and jelly sandwich	440	Small salad with dressing	166
Grilled cheese sandwich	436	Green beans	20
Hamburger with bun	275	Peas	55
Slice of cheese pizza	290	Corn on the cob	123
Taco	210	Broccoli	27
1 orange or apple	85	Tomato soup	161
1 banana	109	Vegetable soup	145
Apple juice	120	Low-fat milk	122

NOTE

Students solve real-world problems involving the math content of this unit.
MWI Solving a Multi-Step Problem

© Pearson Education **3**

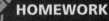
Plan a Meal

 1 Use the food chart to plan a meal. Try to make the total number of calories as close to 800 as you can.

    a. Write an equation to show the total calories.

    b. How close to 800 calories did you get?

 2 Plan a different meal with close to 800 calories.

    a. Write an equation to show the total calories.

    b. How close to 800 calories did you get?

Larger Numbers and Multi-Step Problems

Larger Numbers and
Multi-Step Problems

NAME

DATE

Solving Division Problems

Solve these problems. You may use cubes, grid paper, drawings, or other math tools. Show your work for each problem.

1 Jung has 45 marbles. She wants to put them in groups of 9. How many equal groups can Jung make?

2 Edwin has 21 apples. He is going to use all the apples to make 3 pies. If he uses the same number for each pie, how many apples are in each pie?

3 Mr. Jones has 32 students. He wants to have 8 students in each group. How many groups can he make?

For each problem, write a word problem and then solve.

4 $48 \div 6$

5 $7\overline{)42}$

NAME   DATE

Solving Addition Problems

Solve each problem and show your solution.

 1   821 + 594 = _____

 2   419 + 784 = _____

Write an equation to go with the story problem.

 3   The softball team hit 385 balls during batting practice on Monday, 349 balls on Wednesday, and 415 balls on Friday. How many balls did they hit during the week?

NOTE

Students solve addition problems with 3-digit numbers.
MWI Addition Strategies: Adding One Number in Parts

NAME _____ DATE _____

Multiplication Problems

Show how you solve each problem.

 1 Ladybugs have 6 legs. How many legs do
7 ladybugs have?

 2 An octagon has 8 sides. How many sides are there
on 9 octagons?

3 $4 \times 7 =$ _____

4 Each apple tree has 30 apples on it. How many
apples are on 5 trees?

 5 At the pet store, each aquarium has 60 fish in it.
How many fish are in 4 aquariums?

NOTE _____

Students solve multiplication problems, some involving multiples of 10.
MWI **Multiplying Groups of 10**

NAME

DATE

About the Mathematics in This Unit

Dear Family,

Our class is starting a new unit about multiplication and division called *Larger Numbers and Multi-Step Problems*. During this unit, students build on the work they did in Unit 5. Students solve multiplication and division problems within 100 including multiplication problems in which they multiply a two-digit by a one-digit number, and solve division problems with two-digit quotients. They also solve multi-step problems.

Throughout the unit, students work toward these goals:

Benchmarks	Examples
Solve multiplication and division problems within 100.	Ms. Gomez has 5 boxes of crayons. There are 16 crayons in each box. How many crayons does Ms. Gomez have? $5 \times 10 = 50$ $5 \times 6 = 30$ $30 + 50 = 80$
Demonstrate fluency with the division facts.	$42 \div 7 =$ _____ $42 \div$ _____ $= 7$ Start with $7 \times 5 = 35$
Solve multi-step problems involving more than one operation.	Franick starts with 30 marbles and receives 3 marbles every night. How many marbles does Franick have on Day 10?

About the Mathematics in This Unit

Benchmarks	Examples
Find the area of a rectangular array by breaking it apart (using the distributive property).	8×10=80, 8×3=24, 80+24=104 square units
Solve multiplication and division problems involving masses and volumes.	Phillip has 9 buckets. He fills each of the buckets with 4 liters of water and pours them into an empty aquarium. How many liters of water are now in the aquarium? A block of sandstone has a mass of 72 kilograms. Alicia cuts the block into 8 smaller, same-size blocks. What is the mass of each of the smaller blocks?

This unit is the third of three units in Grade 3 that focus on multiplication and division.

In our math class, students spend time discussing problems in depth and are asked to share their reasoning and solutions. It is most important that children accurately and efficiently solve math problems in ways that make sense to them. At home, encourage your child to explain his or her math thinking to you.

NAME

DATE

Division Facts Practice 1

Write the answers to the following questions as quickly as you can.

$40 \div 8 =$	$100 \div 10 =$	$30 \div 6 =$	$5 \div 5 =$
$25 \div 5 =$	$18 \div 9 =$	$20 \div 5 =$	$30 \div 3 =$
$60 \div 6 =$	$35 \div 5 =$	$4 \div 2 =$	$70 \div 10 =$

Circle any of the problems above that took you more than a few seconds to solve.

Write clues to help you solve them more quickly.

NOTE

Students practice division facts.

MWI **Learning Division Facts**

Related Division Problems

Solve these problems. You may use cubes, grid paper, drawings, or other math tools to help you. Show your thinking for each problem. In each set, try to use the first problem to help you solve the second problem.

1

a. There are 20 first grade students in Mrs. A's class. If she puts them in groups of 4, how many groups will there be?

b. There are 28 second grade students in Mr. B's class. If he puts them in groups of 4, how many groups will there be?

Related Division Problems

2

a. Murphy picked 40 flowers. She wants to give the same number of flowers to 8 friends. How many flowers will each friend get?

b. Adam picked 48 flowers. He wants to give the same number of flowers to 8 friends. How many flowers will each friend get?

Related Division Problems

3   **a.** Gina and Gil were helping Mr. Jones set up for a party. There were 35 chairs and they wanted to put an equal number of chairs at 7 tables. How many chairs will be at each table?

   b. Murphy and Adam were helping Ms. Ruiz set up for a party. There were 56 chairs and they wanted to put an equal number of chairs at 7 tables. How many chairs will be at each table?

4   Write a story problem and solve.

$54 \div 9 =$ _____

NAME

DATE

Division Facts Practice 2

Write the answers to the following questions as quickly as you can.

$35 \div 7 =$	$10 \div 1 =$	$45 \div 9 =$	$15 \div 5 =$
$8 \div 2 =$	$40 \div 5 =$	$18 \div 2 =$	$50 \div 5 =$
$40 \div 10 =$	$16 \div 2 =$	$90 \div 10 =$	$80 \div 8 =$

Circle any of the problems above that took you more than a few seconds to solve.

Write clues to help you solve them more quickly.

NOTE

Students practice division facts.
MWI Learning Division Facts

Multiplication Problems Involving Liquid Volume and Mass

Show how you solve each problem.

1 A small fish tank holds 7 liters of water. There are 30 small fish tanks at the pet store. What is the volume of water in all of the small fish tanks in the store?

2 A bucket holds 4 liters of water. What is the volume of 20 buckets of water?

3 Each car's gas tank holds 60 liters of gasoline. How many liters of gasoline are there in 3 cars?

4 One hot dog bun has a mass of 40 grams. There are 8 buns in a package. What is the mass of all 8 of the hot dog buns?

5 Each egg has a mass of 50 grams. Alice has 5 eggs. What is the mass of all of the eggs?

NOTE

Students solve problems about liquid volume and mass that involve multiplication.
MWI **Measuring Liquid Volume**

NAME

DATE

Related Activities to Try at Home

Dear Family,

The activities described here are related to the mathematics in the unit *Larger Numbers and Multi-Step Problems.* Use the activities to enrich your child's learning experience.

Multiplication and Division Problems in Everyday Situations
Students are solving multiplication and division word problems. Encourage your child to help you solve multiplication and division situations that come up in your daily activities.

○ We have 3 more hours to drive on our trip. There are 60 minutes in each hour. How many more minutes are we going to drive?

○ We are bringing orange slices for the soccer players on your team. We want to give each player on your team 4 orange slices. There are 12 players on your team. How many orange slices do we need?

○ We need 56 forks for the party. The forks come in packages of 8. How many packages do we need to buy?

Learning Division Facts Students are expected to know all of the division facts by the end of third grade. You can help your child practice by using the Division Cards they have prepared at school.

$$42 \div 7 = \underline{\hspace{2cm}}$$
$$42 \div \underline{\hspace{2cm}} = 7$$
Start with $7 \times 5 = 35$

How Did You Solve That? Ask your child to tell you about how he or she is multiplying and dividing. Because these strategies may be unfamiliar to you, listen carefully to your child's explanation; you might even try to do a problem or two using the new procedure.

What Do You Do with the Extras?

Solve each story problem and show your thinking. You may use cubes or drawings to help you. For each problem, decide what to do with the extras and explain your answer.

 1 There are 32 students going on a field trip. Each car holds 5 students. How many cars will they need?

 2 If 4 people share 18 balloons equally, how many balloons will each person get?

What Do You Do with the Extras?

3 Four people share 26 apples equally. How many apples does each person get?

4 There are 60 students going to see a movie. Each row holds 9 people. How many rows can they completely fill up?

5 There are 30 students in the cafeteria. Each table seats 8 students. How many tables do the students need?

Mass and Liquid Volume Problems

Solve the problems. Show your solutions.

1 A grocery store has 250 kilograms of apples and 295 kilograms of oranges. What is the total mass of these fruits?

2 In one day, a grocery store sells 480 kilograms of bananas and 200 kilograms of plantains. What is the mass of the bananas and plantains sold that day?

3 One jar holds 300 milliliters of water. Another jar holds 425 milliliters of water. How many more milliliters of water does the second jar hold?

4 A gas station sold 500 liters of gas one day. The next day, the same gas station sold 475 liters of gas. How much gas did the gas station sell in the two days?

NOTE

Students solve mass and liquid volume problems involving addition and subtraction.
MWI **Measuring Mass**

NAME   DATE

More Division Problems

Solve the problems.

 1 Ms. Smith has 64 apples. She can put 8 apples in each bag. How many bags can she fill?

2 Gina has 27 bottles of water. She wants to give them out equally to 9 of her friends. How many water bottles will each friend get?

3 Edwin has 36 crayons. He gives an equal number to 4 of his friends. How many crayons does each friend get?

4 There are 49 third grade students. The teachers want to split them into 7 equal groups. How many students are in each group?

 5 There are 20 students in Mr. Jones's class. He wants to split them into 5 equal groups. How many students will be in each group?

NOTE

Students solve word problems that involve division.
MWI Solving Division Problems

Division Problems

Solve the problems and show your thinking, including what you decide to do if there are extras left over.

 1 Two people share 15 crackers equally. How many crackers does each person get?

 2 Six friends earned $36 washing people's cars. They want to share the money equally. How much money does each person get?

 3 Three students share 28 pencils equally. How many pencils does each person get?

Division Problems

4 The students from two 3rd grade classes are going on a field trip. There are 43 students. Five students can ride in each car. How many cars are needed?

5 Mrs. Green has 54 oranges and wants to put 9 in each bag. How many bags does she need?

Division Problems

Write a story problem for Problems 6–8, and solve.

6 $40 \div 8 =$ _____

7 $9\overline{)72}$

8 $24 \div 7$

School Supplies

Solve each problem and show your thinking.

 1 Elena had 24 crayons and wanted to put an equal number into 3 boxes. How many crayons are in each box?

 2 Mr. D bought a box of erasers for his class. In the box, there were 7 rows of erasers, with 7 erasers in each row. How many erasers were in the box?

 3 Adam had 30 markers. He wants to loan sets of 5 markers to friends. How many friends can he loan markers to?

School Supplies

4   Oscar had 8 different colors of paper in his notebook. If he has 9 sheets of each color, how many sheets does he have?

5   Ms. E has 28 pairs of scissors. She wants to place an equal number of scissors on 7 different tables. How many scissors can she put on each table?

6   Deondra has 48 jumbo paper clips. She wants to put all the clips into small plastic bags with 6 clips in each bag. How many plastic bags does she need?

NAME

DATE

Division Facts Practice 3

Write the answers to the problems as quickly as you can.

32 ÷ 8 =	24 ÷ 4 =	24 ÷ 3 =	24 ÷ 8 =	48 ÷ 6 =
18 ÷ 3 =	49 ÷ 7 =	21 ÷ 7 =	54 ÷ 9 =	36 ÷ 4 =

Circle any of the problems above that took you more than a few seconds to solve.
Write clues to help you solve them more quickly.

NOTE

Students practice division facts.
MWI **Learning Division Facts**

NAME _____ DATE _____

Liquid Volume, Mass, and Multiplication

Solve each problem. Show how you got your answer.

1 A water jug holds 3 liters of water.
How many liters are there in 8 jugs?

2 A watermelon has a mass of 2 kilograms.
What is the mass of 9 watermelons?

3 Keisha has 7 coins that each have a mass of
5 grams. What is the mass of all the coins?

4 Each day, Ms. Ruiz drinks 2 liters of water.
How much water does she drink in 7 days?

5 $4 \times 6 =$ _____

6 $5 \times 9 =$ _____

NOTE

Students solve multiplication problems including some word problems about liquid
volume and mass.
MWI Solving Multiplication Problems

NAME

DATE

Division Facts Practice 4

Write the answers to the problems as quickly as you can.

$42 \div 7 =$	$36 \div 6 =$	$64 \div 8 =$	$72 \div 8 =$	$54 \div 6 =$
$12 \div 3 =$	$63 \div 9 =$	$16 \div 4 =$	$27 \div 9 =$	$56 \div 7 =$

Circle any of the problems above that took you more than a few seconds to solve.

Write clues to help you solve them more quickly.

NOTE

Students practice division facts.

MWI Learning Division Facts

Solving Multiplication Problems

Solve the problems and show your solutions.

 There are 4 teams playing soccer at the park. There are 23 people on each team. How many people are playing soccer?

2 There are 11 people on each basketball team. How many people are on 6 teams?

 Ms. Santos sells bags of oranges at her store. There are 8 oranges in each bag. Becky bought 12 bags of oranges. How many oranges did she buy?

Solving Multiplication Problems

 A pentagon has 5 sides. How many sides are on 15 pentagons?

 Ms. Ruiz bought 3 packages of napkins for a party. Each package contains 38 napkins. How many napkins did she buy?

6 Ms. Santos has 9 bags of apples. There are 17 apples in each bag. How many apples does Ms. Santos have?

Solving Multiplication Problems

Write story problems for 7 and 8, and solve.

7   15 × 8 = _____

8   4 × 26 = _____

Division Facts Practice 5

Write the answers to the problems as quickly as you can.

56 ÷ 8 =	42 ÷ 6 =	18 ÷ 6 =	72 ÷ 9 =	27 ÷ 3 =
36 ÷ 9 =	28 ÷ 7 =	48 ÷ 8 =	81 ÷ 9 =	63 ÷ 7 =

Circle any of the problems above that took you more than a few seconds to solve.
Write clues to help you solve them more quickly.

NOTE

Students practice solving division facts.
MWI Learning Division Facts

NAME _____ DATE _____

Solving More Multiplication Problems

Solve each problem. Show your solution.

1 A package of crackers has 12 crackers. Adam buys 5 packages. How many crackers does he have?

2 There are 30 oranges on each tree. How many oranges are on 4 trees?

3 A book has 8 chapters. Each chapter has 20 pages. How many pages are in the book?

4 There are 6 groups of students. Each group has 14 students. How many students are there?

5 $16 \times 7 =$ _____

6 $14 \times 8 =$ _____

7 $50 \times 3 =$ _____

8 $17 \times 4 =$ _____

NOTE

Students multiply 2-digit numbers by 1-digit numbers.
MWI Solving Multiplication Problems

Using Arrays

Label the dimensions of each of the arrays.
Find the area, and show how you found it.

1

2

Using Arrays

3

4

Using Arrays

5

6

Our Collections

For each problem, write an equation that represents the problem, solve the problem, and show your solution.

 Deondra collects coins. She had 385 coins in her collection. On her birthday, her uncle gave her 125 more coins to add to her collection. How many coins does Deondra have now?

 Oscar collects comic books. He has 462 superhero comic books and 394 cartoon comic books. How many comic books does he have altogether?

NOTE

Students solve addition and subtraction problems in a story problem context.
MWI Addition Strategies: Adding by Place

© Pearson Education 3

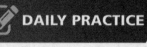
Our Collections

 3 Nancy collects toy cars. She had 429 in her collection. She sold 180 of them to a friend. How many toy cars does Nancy have left?

4 Adam collects flag stickers. He had 534 in his collection. He gave away 172 of them to the history teacher. How many flag stickers does Adam have left?

NAME

DATE

Multiplying with Arrays

Label the dimensions of each of the arrays.
Find the area, and show how you found it.

 1

2

NOTE

Students find the product of arrays with one dimension greater than 10.
MWI Using Arrays to Solve Multiplication Problems

UNIT 8 | **499** | SESSION 2.2

© Pearson Education 3

Multiplying with Arrays

Division Problems

Solve the problems and show your solutions, including what you decided to do if there were extras left over.

 1 There are 39 first graders on the playground. The teacher wants to put them in groups of 3. How many groups can he make?

2 There are 78 fourth grade students. The teachers want to put the students into 5 equal groups. How many students are in each group?

3 There are 86 second graders. The teachers want to put them in groups of 4. How many groups can the teachers make?

Division Problems

4   Mrs. Smith has 8 bags of apples. There are
104 apples altogether. If the apples are divided
evenly, how many apples are in each bag?

5   Mr. Jones has 93 oranges. He wants to put the
oranges into 6 bags, with an equal number of
oranges in each bag. How many oranges will be
in each bag?

6   Ms. Walker has 98 lemons. She wants to put
the lemons in 7 bags, with an equal number of
lemons in each bag. How many lemons will be
in each bag?

Division Problems

Write a story problem for 7–10 and solve.

7   99 ÷ 9 = _____

8   84 ÷ 4 = _____

9   8)128

10   115 ÷ 5 = _____

ACTIVITY

Multiplication Problems

Solve the problems and show your solutions.

 1 Ladybugs have 6 legs. How many legs are on 22 ladybugs?

 2 There are 9 players on each softball team. How many players are on 12 teams?

3 Ms. Gomez has 5 boxes of crayons. There are 16 crayons in each box. How many crayons does Ms. Gomez have?

 4 A family pack has 18 frozen juice bars. How many juice bars are in 3 packs?

Solve:

5 $17 \times 6 =$ _____

6 $21 \times 8 =$ _____

7 $28 \times 3 =$ _____

Multiplication Problems

Label the dimensions of each of the arrays. Find the area of each array, and show how you found it.

8

9

10

NAME _____ DATE _____

Money Problems

Solve the following problems and show your solutions.

 1 $5.67 + $4.98 = _____

 2 $7.43 + $3.87 = _____

 3 $6.80 − $2.95 = _____

4 $8.25 − $5.27 = _____

NOTE

Students solve addition and subtraction problems, using the context of money.

MWI Subtraction Strategies: Adding Up and Subtracting Back

Solving Multi-Step Problems

Solve the problems and show your solutions.

1. There are four 3rd grade classes with different numbers of students in each class: 22, 23, 25, and 26. The teachers put all the classes together and made 6 equal groups. How many students are in each group?

2. One day at the store, Dwayne buys 3 cases of water. A case has 24 bottles. His 4 sons share the water equally. How many bottles of water does each son get?

3. There are 9 flowers in each bunch. On Monday, Murphy bought 8 bunches. On Wednesday, she bought 5 bunches. How many flowers did Murphy buy?

Solving Multi-Step Problems

4 Mrs. G has 104 oranges. She used 8 to make orange juice, and put the remaining ones into 4 bags. She put an equal number in each bag. How many oranges are in each bag?

5 At the park there were people and dogs. Each person has 2 legs, and each dog has 4 legs. If there were 100 legs at the park, how many people and dogs could there be? Find as many solutions as you can.

NAME _____ DATE _____

Subtraction Story Problems

Solve each problem and show your solution.

1 A medium pizza costs $9.49 and a small pizza costs $7.85. How much more is a medium pizza than a small pizza?

2 Barney had 605 postcards in his collection. He gave 136 postcards to his younger sister so that she could start her own collection. How many postcards does Barney have now?

3 Mr. Gillespie's class goal is to collect 1,350 signatures for the petition. So far the students have collected 968 signatures. How many more signatures do they need to meet their goal?

NOTE

Students solve subtraction problems with 3-digit numbers.
MWI Subtraction Strategies: Subtracting One Number in Parts

NAME _____ DATE _____

Solving More Division Problems

Solve the problems and show your solutions, including what you decide to do if there are extras left over.

 1 Elena had 81 grapes. She wanted to give an equal number of grapes to each of her 9 friends. How many grapes did each friend get?

2 There are 80 third grade students. The teachers want to split them into groups of 3. How many groups will there be?

3 The library just received 102 books. The librarian wants to make 4 piles of books with the same number of books in each pile. How many books will be in each pile?

4 Zhang has 112 crayons. He wants to separate them into groups of 7. How many groups will he have?

Write a word problem for Problems 5–6 and solve.

5 120 ÷ 6

6 79 ÷ 3

 NOTE
_____

Students solve division problems. Some of the problems have remainders.
MWI Remainders: What Do You Do With the Extras?

NAME

DATE

Solving Subtraction Problems

Solve each problem and show your solution. For the story problem, write an equation to go with the problem.

1 713 − 461 = _____

2 $8.43 − $5.95 = _____

3 Pete, a western lowland gorilla, weighs 411 pounds. Nina, his mate, weighs 263 pounds. How much heavier is Pete than Nina?

NOTE

Students solve subtraction problems with 3-digit numbers.
MWI Subtraction Situations

More Multi-Step Problems

Solve the problems and show your solutions.

1 Jane has 3 bags of apples. Each bag has a different number of apples: 12, 13, 15. She wants to split them into 5 equal groups. How many apples will be in each group?

2 Each bag has 10 oranges. Adam buys 8 bags and wants to split the oranges between 4 friends. How many oranges does each friend get?

3 There are 12 pens in each box. On Tuesday, Dwayne bought 4 boxes of pens. On Friday, he went back to the store and bought 3 more boxes. How many pens did Dwayne buy?

4 Ms. Smith's class is planting a garden. There are 21 students in her class. She splits the class into groups of 3. Each group plants 2 packets of seeds. How many packets of seeds did the class plant?

5 Each of the 4th grade classes has 20 students. There are 4 classes. The teachers want to split the students into groups of 8. How many groups will there be?

NOTE

Students solve multi-step problems involving more than one operation.
MWI Solving a Multi-Step Problem

NAME

DATE

Franick's Marbles

Franick had 30 Magic Marbles left from the year before. She was then given 3 Magic Marbles on the first night, 3 more Magic Marbles on the second night, 3 more Magic Marbles on the third night, and so on, for 20 nights.

Make a representation—a diagram or picture—that shows how the number of Franick's Magic Marbles changes. Someone looking at your representation should be able to tell the number of marbles Franick has on any day.

Bolar's Marbles

Bolar had no Magic Marbles left from the year before. He was then given 5 Magic Marbles on the first night, 5 more Magic Marbles on the second night, 5 more Magic Marbles on the third night, and so on, for 20 nights.

Make a representation—a diagram or picture—that shows how the number of Bolar's Magic Marbles changes. Someone looking at your representation should be able to tell the number of marbles Bolar has on any day.

NAME _____   DATE _____

Practice with Addition

Solve each problem and show your solution. For the story problem, write an equation to go with the problem.

1   826 + 358 = _____

2   763 + 429 = _____

3   539 + 620 = _____

4   For the past three weeks, Beatriz has been keeping track of how many pages she reads. The first week, she read 325 pages. During the second week, she read 217 pages. The third week, she read 240 pages. How many total pages did she read?

NOTE

Students add 3-digit numbers.

MWI Addition Strategies: Adding One Number in Parts

NAME   DATE

Multiplication and Division Problems

Solve each problem. Show your solution.

 Ms. Smith bought a sheet of stickers. There are 7 rows with 11 stickers in each row. How many stickers are on the sheet?

 There are 67 students outside. The teachers want to split the students into 4 equal groups. How many students will be in each group?

 Each basketball team has 5 players. There are 9 teams. How many basketball players are on all of the teams?

 There are 80 plates in a cabinet. There are 4 different sizes of plates. There are the same number of each size plate. How many plates are there of each size?

NOTE

Students solve multiplication and division problems.
MWI Solving Division Problems

Table for Franick and Bolar

Day	Franick	Bolar
Beginning Amount	30	0
1		
2		
3		
4		
5		
6		
7		
8		
9		
10		

Table for Franick and Bolar

Day	Franick	Bolar
11		
12		
13		
14		
15		
16		
17		
18		
19		
20		

Rules for Franick and Bolar

Franick starts with 30 marbles and receives 3 marbles every night.

Bolar starts with no marbles and receives 5 marbles every night.

 Figure out how many marbles Bolar has on Day 10 without looking at your table.

 Figure out how many marbles Franick has on Day 10 without looking at your table.

 Write in words a rule for figuring out how many marbles Bolar has on any day.

4 Write in words a rule for figuring out how many marbles Franick has on any day.

NAME _____ DATE _____

What is Your Favorite Food?

Some people were asked, "What is your favorite food?" Their responses were used to make a bar graph of the data. Use the bar graph to answer the questions below.

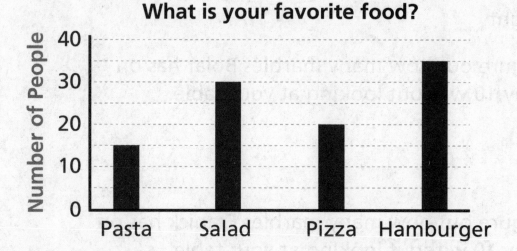

What is your favorite food?

1. How many people picked pizza as their favorite food?

2. How many people participated in the survey?

3. How many fewer people picked pizza than picked salad?

4. How many more people picked hamburger than picked pasta?

NOTE

Students answer questions and solve problems about a bar graph.
MWI Describing and Summarizing Data

Table for Zupin and Tovar

Day	Zupin	Tovar
Beginning Amount	20	30
1		
2		
3		
4		
5		
6		
7		
8		
9		
10		

Table for Zupin and Tovar

Day	Zupin	Tovar
11		
12		
13		
14		
15		
16		
17		
18		
19		
20		

Rules for Zupin and Tovar

Zupin starts with 20 marbles and receives 4 marbles every night.

Tovar starts with 30 marbles and receives 4 marbles every night.

1 Figure out how many marbles Zupin and Tovar each have on Day 16 without looking at your table.

2 Figure out how many marbles Zupin and Tovar each have on Day 19 without looking at your table.

3 Write in words a rule for figuring out how many marbles Zupin has on any day.

4 Write in words a rule for figuring out how many marbles Tovar has on any day.

NAME

DATE

Multiplying and Dividing with Liquid Volume and Mass

Solve each problem. Show your solution.

 1. Oscar has 64 liters of water. He divides the water equally among 8 buckets. What is the volume of water in each of the buckets?

 2. Edwin has 7 tiles, each with the same mass. The total mass of the tiles is 56 grams. What is the mass of each tile?

3. Ms. R has 18 liters of juice. She pours all of it into 6 bottles, with the same amount in each bottle. How many liters are in each bottle?

 4. A bakery has 42 kilograms of flour. The baker wants to divide the flour into containers and put 7 kilograms of flour in each container. How many containers will she need?

NOTE

Students use multiplication and division to solve word problems about liquid volume and mass.

MWI Solving Division Problems

© Pearson Education 3

Etaan's Marbles

Etaan starts with 10 marbles and receives 3 marbles every night.

1 Figure out how many marbles Etaan has on each of the first 10 days.

Day	Etaan's Total Marbles
Beginning Amount	10
1	
2	
3	
4	
5	
6	
7	
8	
9	
10	

NOTE

Students solve multi-step problems and come up with a rule for determining answers to the problems.

Etaan's Marbles

 Figure out how many marbles Etaan has on Day 15.

 Figure out how many marbles Etaan has on Day 22.

 Write a rule for figuring out how many marbles Etaan has on any day.

NOTE

Students solve multi-step problems and come up with a rule for determining answers to the problems.

MWI **Writing Rules**

NAME

DATE

Equations for Marble Problems

1 This equation is about Zupin's marbles:

$Z = 20 + (18 \times 4)$

What does Z mean?

What does the 20 represent?

What does the 18 represent?

2 This equation is about Tovar's marbles:

$30 + (4 \times D) = T$

What does T mean?

What does D mean?

What does the 30 represent?

What does the 4 represent?

Marble Problems with 30 Days

In one of the towns on Rhomaar, children get marbles for the first 30 nights of the year. Here is the information for two of those children.

Ferben starts with 10 Magic Marbles and gets 4 each night.

Sujor starts with 0 Magic Marbles and gets 4 each night.

 Write an equation for how many marbles Ferben has on Day 15. Use *F* to stand for Ferben's total marbles.

 Write an equation for how many marbles Sujor has on Day 15. Use *S* to stand for Sujor's total marbles.

Marble Problems with 30 Days

3   Ferben and Sujor are comparing their marbles on Day 15. Who has more marbles? How many more? Show or explain how you figured this out.

4   Ferben and Sujor compare again on Day 29. Who has more marbles? How many more? Show or explain how you figured this out.

NAME _____ DATE _____

Rules for Finding Total Marbles

1 Write a rule or directions for how to figure out how many Magic Marbles Ferben has on any day. Write an equation to go with your rule. Use *F* to stand for the total number of marbles Ferben has.

2 Write a rule or directions for how to figure out how many Magic Marbles Sujor has on any day. Write an equation to go with your rule. Use *S* to stand for the total number of marbles Sujor has.

Find the Unknown Amount

Solve the problems and show your thinking.

 Winger gets 5 marbles every night. On Day 15, she has 95 marbles. How many Magic Marbles did she save from last year?

 Jorad saved 20 marbles from last year. On Day 10, she has 80 marbles. How many Magic Marbles does she get each night?

3 Gowen gets 6 marbles every night. On Day 19, he has 114 marbles. How many Magic Marbles did he save from last year?

NAME   DATE

Comparing Fractions

Compare the fractions in each problem. Use pictures of brownies or number lines to show how you know which fraction is greater. Record your solution by using <, >, or = to compare the fractions.

1   Chris ate $\frac{3}{4}$ of a brownie. Becky ate $\frac{3}{8}$ of a brownie. Who ate more? Or did they eat the same amount? Show how you know.

2   Jane walked $\frac{5}{8}$ of a mile. Gil walked $\frac{2}{8}$ of a mile. Who walked farther? Or did they walk the same distance? Show how you know.

3   Kim drank $\frac{3}{6}$ of a glass of water. Edwin drank $\frac{3}{8}$ of a glass of water. Who drank more water? Or did they drink the same amount? Show how you know.

4   Compare $\frac{3}{4}$ and $\frac{6}{8}$. Which fraction is greater? Or are the fractions equal? Show how you know.

NOTE

Students compare fractions with the same numerator or denominator.
MWI **Comparing Fractions with the Same Numerator or Denominator**

NAME   DATE

More Practice with Multi-Step Problems

Solve each problem. Show your solution.

 1   There are four 3rd grade classes. Each class has 24 students. The teachers want to split all the students evenly into 3 groups. How many students will be in each group?

2   There are 3 groups of students. One group has 12 students, the next has 14, and the last has 16. If each student gets 3 cookies, how many cookies are there altogether?

3   There are 5 frogs in the pond. 8 more hop over. Each frog has 4 spots. How many spots are there on all the frogs?

4   There are 10 ladybugs. Three have 8 spots, 4 have 12 spots, and 3 have 10 spots. How many spots are on all the ladybugs?

5   Deondra has 3 bags of apples: one with 10 apples, one with 13 apples, and one with 14 apples. She wants to give them all out equally to 6 of her friends. How many apples will each friend get?

NOTE

Students solve multi-step problems involving more than one operation.
MWI Solving a Multi-Step Problem

NAME   DATE

Practice with Multiplication and Division Problems

Solve each problem. Show your solution.

1 Arthur and his friends washed cars. They used 5 buckets of water. Each bucket held 15 liters of water. How many liters of water did they use?

2 There are 28 tennis balls. Each container holds 4 tennis balls. How many containers will be filled?

3 There are 12 grapes on each bunch. Keisha buys 5 bunches of grapes and wants to split them among 4 people. How many grapes does each person get?

4 There are 25 balloons. Nicholas wants to give the balloons equally to 6 people. How many balloons does each person get?

NOTE

Students solve multiplication and division story problems.
MWI **Solving Multiplication Problems**